# THE FRUITS OF WISDOM

**Kervin Dieudonne**
**Biblical Principles, Wisdom, Understanding & Life Principles**

All rights reserved
Copyright © 2024 by Kervin Dieudonne

No part of this publication may be reproduced, distributed, or transmitted in any form or by any means, including photocopying, recording, or other electronic or mechanical methods, without the prior written permission of the publisher, except in the case of brief quotations embodied in critical reviews and certain other noncommercial uses permitted by copyright law.

Published by Spines
ISBN: 979-8-89383-694-3

# THE FRUITS OF WISDOM

"LIFE AND BIBLE"

PROPHET DR. KERVIN DIEUDONNE

# PREFACE

Greetings,

Quite often, I'm asked to share how I've navigated the challenging path of life and ministry. In the pages of this book, I hope to share with you the invaluable lessons I have learned and the profound insights I have gained along the way.

Throughout my many years of serving in various capacities within the ministry, I have faced countless trials and tribulations. These experiences have not only tested my faith, but have also served as powerful catalysts for growth and transformation. Each trial, no matter how difficult, has been an opportunity for God to teach me something profound about His character and His plans for my life.

It is through these teachings that I have come to realize the depth of God's love and His unwavering faithfulness. I have learned that even in the darkest of times, when all hope seems lost, God is never absent; rather, He is using those very trials to refine and shape me into the person He intends for me to be.

The wisdom and understanding gained from these experiences have proven to be invaluable in my journey as a servant of God. It has equipped me with the discernment to make sound decisions, the resilience to face adversity head-on, and the compassion to minister to those in need. It is my hope that by sharing these lessons with you, you too will be inspired and encouraged to persevere through your own trials and discover the incredible growth that comes from them.

As we embark on this journey together, I invite you to open your heart and mind to the transformative power of God's teachings. May the lessons shared within these pages ignite a fire within you, propelling you towards a deeper relationship with our heavenly Father and a greater understanding of His divine plans for your life.

So, let us dive into the depths of wisdom and understanding that can only be found through the trials and teachings of our loving God. Through vulnerability and reflection, may you find inspiration, encouragement, and the courage to embrace the challenges that lie ahead. And may you, like me, discover that the trials we face are not meant to break us but to mold us into vessels of His grace and love.

With Wisdom and Love,

**Prophet Dr. Kervin Dieudonne**

# BIBLICAL QUOTES AND LIFE QUOTES

〜

1. The Bible is a mirror. See yourself first in it.

2. Be careful and test the spirit. Wisdom always wins over folly.

3. The true power of God is when you accept everyone as God's children with no partiality.

4. Every man is infected with that disease called sin. The only thing that prevents this disease from killing somebody is the blood of Jesus Christ.

5. God is not a coward. He took full responsibility for his creation's failure to obey him by giving Jesus Christ the right to die for the world. You are free. You just have not claimed it yet. You are saved. You just have not claimed it yet. You are justified. You just have not

claimed it yet. Many more... Claim your total restoration.

6. Knowledge doesn't need a good heart to get it; anyone can be informed and educated, good or bad.

7. The thing with wisdom is that once you become bitter, she leaves you.

8. We preach as if hell has a connection with heaven, but earth is the connection to heaven.

9. Sheep love victory and hate suffering.

10. Shepherds love the process of suffering; rest in victory.

11. Jesus didn't have money, but He never said he was broke, yet he withdrew from the fish's mouth, the richest of heaven.

12. No one goes to the house of God and comes back empty-handed.

13. The cost of righteousness is free, but the cost of being a good person will cost you your life.

14. If your serving has tricks in it, your ministry or destiny will be tricky.

If your serving has an interest in it, your destiny and ministry will come with interest.

If your serving has lies in it, your ministry and destiny will be full of lies.

If you are true to your serving, your destiny and ministry will be the real deal.

The results of your serving will be the outcome of your life or destiny.

15. Submission is a powerful thing; literally, it holds a lot of power for the person who is above and the person who is submitting. Those of you who don't understand that and can't submit are the reason why a lot of things don't work for you.

16. Submission power is determined by the position, level, or rank of the person. You can't submit to someone under you because the power is above.

17. Submission of a church member to a church leader is in the position. Submission of a wife to her husband is in the position. You don't submit to the person, but to the position.

18. If you can't submit, it means you don't respect the person, which means the power of the position will never work for you.

19. The position of the person is not just a title; it comes through hard work and sweat. It's a level of

success and achievement. So, if you want to grow, you must submit to it in order to grow.

20. Wisdom is the science of heaven. It has answers to all.

21. There are people who are sent. There are people who went.

22. If God does not draw you, you cannot come near Him.

23. If you have to be chosen, God will send Samuel.

24. There are many crowns we will receive when we meet with the Lord. The crowns are achievements.

25. When you endure the things of life and the suffering of this life, which is the only way you can receive the crown of life, accept to go through the process.

26. Every time you run away from your issues or problems, you are telling the Lord to dismiss the crowns of life.

27. This is why the devil doesn't like you. You were born blessed. You were created blessed. Everything you do is blessed.

28. The Word of God cannot expire because He is I Am, not I Was.

29. There are certain times you get in the presence of God; you need to give God a Barak praise—a praise of reverence.

30. Sight is attracted by the sower.

31. A prophet you sow into will see and hear for you from the Lord.

32. Humility comes with boldness. Confidence comes with self-respect, not shyness.

33. Someone who can't confess the moment of their stupidity is someone who believes they are stupidly smart.

34. Whatever you decide to do in life, if you learn to understand its suffering, you will be successful.

35. When God is going to do it for you, no one or nothing will be able to stop you. Your season is your season.

36. The Bible has a voice. When you build a relationship with your Bible, that's when the Bible speaks to you.

37. How did God provide the seed to the sower? He planted the tree, and the sower picked the seed. The sower didn't have a tree to get the seed from. God

made the trees before he made man. He provided the seeds to the sower.

38. The church is trying to create a system based on their perspectives on others, not the revelation of the Spirit, but God calling who he wants and teaching them how he wants. Don't be like the scribes and the Pharisees.

39. The power is in God; if you want it, the attention should be on Christ Jesus. He knows the way, and He is the way.

40. There are true holy men of God who are separate and do only God's will and God's work.

41. God is more than a vault or a storehouse for you to be blessed. He is your salvation and eternal redemption.

42. Religion is what killed Jesus. Freedom of religion is what raised him from the dead.

43. If heaven isn't real, talk about your place of rest after leaving this world. If you don't know, keep your mouth shut.

44. If your God is the true God, prove it in power. The kingdom of God is not a matter of talk but of power.

45. If you don't believe in the Bible, stop trying to prove it is false. No one throws stones at a mad man. No one gives value to something that's fake. You're giving it a lot of value, but yet you say you don't believe in it. Talk about what you believe in, not what you don't believe in. If you don't believe in Jesus, stop mentioning his name. If you're against him, you can't be with him.

46. Prophesying to a prideful or egocentric person is like telling a murderer it's ok to kill people.

47. God is not a source of belief to control the world. He is a source of belief that controls the world. No one forces me to believe in God. He already had me.

48. You are a light to the world. You have met a man named Jesus. Your light can no longer be hidden. Preach, for it is still daytime. The Lord is with you.

49. Ministry is not something I know I can do; it's something you were (Called) (Anointed) (Sent) to do.

50. If your house looks more presentable than the temple of God, you are a thief. You have not entered through the gate.

51. Christians, preachers, and church folks... You don't need to be the best. You just have to do your best. That's all. We don't do things like the world does. The

only greatest of all time we have is Jesus—past, present, and future.

52. Church people will tell you that God is the head of the church. But they are controlling everyone, and they never heard a word God said. We need to listen to the Holy Spirit, not ourselves.

53. Most of the time, it's the small churches that received the prophetic with an open heart that brought a move of God. The big churches are too busy looking important; even when you're speaking the word of the Lord to them, they feel embarrassed because they feel too important.

54. Church is the place where you find character assassins, just because you want to do something good with your life. But if you are doing badly, they encourage you to do something good. Come on, make up your mind, or we need the Holy Spirit.

55. Church people will tell you God is the head of the church, but they are controlling everyone, and they never heard a word God said. We need the Holy Spirit.

56. When it comes to church people, if they are not sure they are going to heaven, they will look for something against you to show you're not qualified to go to heaven because of their uncertainty. We need the Holy Spirit.

57. Church people want you to stay close to God, yet they will push you away from God. We need the Holy Spirit.

58. Church people will tell you they don't hate, but they have a list of people they hate and won't let go of. We need the Holy Spirit.

59. Church people will call you a prophet today; when they don't want you anymore, they begin to call you a witch. The same mouth... We need the Holy Spirit.

60. Church people will take you in now for salvation, and when they finish using you, they will kick you out like a dog. We need the Holy Spirit.

61. Church people will lift you up with a good name, and when they can't control you anymore, they will dirty your name. We need the Holy Spirit.

62. I don't understand church people. They will pray and fast for God to save you. They will fast for 21 or 40 days for your salvation. They will spend all night praying for you and for God to deliver you. They will do all that only to throw you under the bus when they find out your sins. The church is the only place they will sacrifice to help you now and destroy you later. That's why we need the Holy Spirit. He is beyond the church.

63. What makes you different? Noah built an ark where there was no rain. While they were laughing at him, he kept building. Doing something that God said to you that's never been done before is different!

64. The level of your obedience is what will cause you to grow.

65. Some of us will enter the Kingdom, while some of us will inherit the Kingdom.

66. If you know the presence of God, you don't need a feeling from your gut to guess things around you.

67. Sometimes we look at persecution as if it is a burden, but persecution is trying to help you grow. You would never have known what God was able to do until you were persecuted.

68. People will always be full of themselves without Christ. Only Jesus can humble them. He is the key to eternal life.

69. Jesus is not just our God. He is our completion. He will make us whole.

70. Why are you hiding? Who told you it's nighttime and you cannot preach the word of God? No, it is daylight. You lock yourself up in a room out of fear. Get out and preach the word of Jesus Christ. It's daylight.

71. You must deny yourself and pick up your cross. Are there people who still believe in that? I'm calling out to you. Preach! It's still daylight. Nighttime has not yet come.

72. Proclaim your faith. Sin enters through one man. Salvation is given through one man. Preach the truth, and don't be afraid. It's still daylight.

73. It's still daylight. Preach! Nighttime has not yet come. Preach Jesus Christ was crucified, died, and resurrected, and yes, we will be caught up in the air on the day of the Lord.

74. The kingdom of God cannot be shaken and will not be shaken. Be proud to be a follower of Jesus Christ. Proclaim your faith. Do not hide it.

75. Don't be afraid. If something was going to happen to you, it would have happened already. God never gave them permission. They are putting up a front to make you afraid. If God is before you, who can be against you?

76. As long as the Holy Spirit is here, don't be afraid. Your wisdom will exceed the wisdom of the scribes and magicians.

77. God can call you and choose you but never claim you. When He claims you, He expresses Himself

concerning you. David, a man according to my heart. Moses, I made you a god. Moses, I spoke face to face. Jesus, my begotten Son. Those are the expressions of God concerning those he claims.

78. Most people who will be making it in the Lord's house are people who are not expected to. The ones that are expected to have denied the invitation to the wedding a long time ago.

79. If you believe it's a fairy tale that Daniel or the lions weren't real, a man couldn't survive it. Your god must be weak, or whatever you believe in is weak.

80. The ability to prophesy the future as a prophet is not to see the unknown (impossible). It is to see the known that has not yet manifested and call it out. That's from the future.

81. The God I serve is not the work of man. He is God all by Himself. He is very invisible, but the chosen ones can see Him, and they speak of Him and preach in His name.

82. A time for everything—a time to lose and a time to win. The Lord spoke to me this morning, saying, "Your time has come to win. You have been losing long enough."

83. If someone says Jesus is not real, they are damming their own souls. I'm not talking about the Jesus they made up and are speaking of. I'm talking about the Jesus who appears to people and reveals Himself in glory.

84. You don't need a mountain of faith to move a mustard seed. But you can have a mustard seed of faith that will move mountains.

85. The other gods know the living God, and they fear Him.

86. When God is sending help to you, He is not going to follow your plan. He has His own way. Israel cried for help. The help was in Pharaoh's house the whole time, observing. A boy killed a giant champion with a rock. A man with superhuman strength and an undisciplined womanizer named Samson destroyed the Philistines while he was blind. The King of Kings and Lord of Lords was born in a barnyard, yet He is God, the Savior of the world. A drunkard by the name of Noah was used to extend humanity because righteousness was found in him. God doesn't follow human plans. He has His own.

87. How do you believe in fortune cookies, fortune tellers, readings of the zodiac, reading numbers, and calling others false prophets?

88. I was born to believe in something, and thank God it was Jesus that became my faith. I'm not better, but the grace of God led me to Jesus.

89. We accuse each other. Then, when it's you personally, you each believe in the grace and mercy of God for you. That's why neither of us is the judge. We all fall short of His glory.

90. The greatest power in the gospel is when you hear a message and you come in agreement with the spoken word. Power will manifest.

91. There is a level when you believe in God. There is a level to having faith in God. There is a level at which you know God.

92. It's not everyone who can speak to your demon, and they listen. Some people will feed your demons, but some will cast them out for you. By the way, even pigs didn't want demons inside them. Mark 5:13

93. If you do not understand Jesus' death, you will never see His resurrection.

94. You have to allow some things to go and live your life so you can see the glory of Jesus Christ.

95. God has no form. Only Jesus can see Him. Jesus is the revelation of God.

96. There's a difference between seeing the Lord and being in His presence.

97. Most church folks want you to buy grace from them. But in their advertisement (preaching), they say it's free.

98. The religion war is scary out there. Everyone wants to be right. Signs of the last days.

99. Tune in to the frequency of heaven. There's always good news for your soul.

100. Prayer is the best Google research a Christian can have. The Spirit searches our hearts.

101. It's a blessing when people hate on you for the sake of righteousness.

102. A relationship with God means He manifests Himself to you everywhere you are.

103. Learn to give to people who are preaching the gospel. You will know them by their fruits.

104. Most people are waiting until you die to honor you. That's why you must embrace Christ Jesus and glorify Him for the crown He will give you, which is worth more than anything anyone could honor you with.

105. Be careful with the people who always want to expose the log in people's eyes but get offended when you speak of the specks in their eyes. Hypocrites they are.

106. If you are infecting people instead of impacting them, stop preaching. Jesus came to cure them, not destroy them.

107. If you don't know Christ Jesus for yourself, you will not understand His preaching and teachings. Get to know Him.

108. Just because you don't want to go to church doesn't stop God from continuing to be God. Just because you don't want to worship doesn't stop God from receiving worship.

109. The worst thing to do is to challenge God. He will defend Himself. On that part, He is not as quiet as you think or as slow as you believe. He will defend Himself.

110. Just because you love the Father does not mean the Son is jealous. Just because you love the Son does not mean the Father is jealous. But it is with jealousy that He gives us the Holy Spirit.

111. The universe is not God. This universe is not the only existing one. There are billions or trillions more. They are all God's creations. If it is created, then it is

not from God. If there are others like it, it is not God. There is only one God, and He manifests Himself as Jesus Christ, so we may know Him and understand a little about Him, and that is the word of God.

112. God proved Himself to be God when He showed humanity that He has an infinite number of ideas or ways of creating when He made each one of us (an infinite number of people) with our own DNA or fingerprint that is not identical.

113. When you are going through your trials, you have to accept. Ask God to bless those who don't like you. Pass the test!

114. God doesn't sit down to think about your next move. He doesn't worry about tomorrow because God is tomorrow.

115. Beauty does not have a face, the same way God doesn't have a face. Anything can be beautiful.

116. God cannot predict the future; you can predict the future. God has already written your whole life. If He already wrote your whole life, what is the future for Him?

117. It doesn't matter who you are today; it was already written by God who you would become because your life is already written.

118. God is not writing your story as you live. He wrote your story before you came. Your destiny is already written. God already knows the plans He has for you.

119. Your destiny is already written. God already knows the plans He has for you.

120. If you want to be free, you must be willing to give God a sacrifice.

121. There's no need to try; if God says it, do it!

122. There's a sacrifice that must come out of you for you to become who God called you to be.

123. The gospel is not what you wear. It's not your outside appearance. It's a sacrifice on the inside.

124. Our job is not to say who will be judged or who will be condemned. Our job is to say Jesus loves you.

125. We were never called to preach against people. We were called to preach the gospel.

126. Oftentimes, we blame God for what He's not giving us. But we are not emptying ourselves to receive what He has for us.

127. Certain things, you have to get them out of you. If you don't, you won't be fit for the blessing God is ready to pour out on you.

BIBLICAL QUOTES AND LIFE QUOTES | 19

128. Whenever God gives you something, He will give you principles and ordinances to keep it.

129. When God tells you He will do something, He'll do it, but you need to align yourself with the word of God.

130. God doesn't tell the future; He is the future.

131. Everything God tells us to do has a reason behind it.

132. There were some strong things fighting against your life, and God delivered you. Yet you still doubt Him.

133. When I have faith, I'm walking on air. The world doesn't see my foundation, and they can't see where I'm going.

134. I don't have any power. I'm just a vessel. I'm just a messenger.

135. The faith of a Christian doesn't need to prove anything.

136. Being a Christian is not like working at Walmart. You can't quit whenever you feel like it. You don't take breaks whenever you feel like it. You need to die to be a Christian.

137. Your title as a Christian is not for you to look good. We overcome the world. You can't run. So, when the fire comes, you need to stand.

138. When you are in Christ, you're already dead. Whatever you do is not for yourself.

139. Faith cannot be activated where there's fear. Don't worry about what they say. What God says matters.

140. As long as the Holy Spirit is here, God will make a way where there seems to be no way.

141. As long as the Holy Spirit is here, the power of God will be shown in demonstration.

142. As Christians, we are the ones who are supposed to make a difference in the world.

143. It's not the prayer; it's the connection with God that gives you power.

144. Prayer is an opportunity to feel the presence of God.

145. God's presence is everywhere. Nothing can hinder the presence of God.

146. Do not size down God in your human mind. He is not a big God. He is God.

147. When you fear God, He will make Himself known to you. When God reveals Himself to you, you have no choice but to worship Him. The fear of God will give you a better flow to worship Him.

148. Just something to think about... Before God, what was there? It was God Himself who was there.

149. Jesus is the answer.

150. Learn to read the bible for yourself. Stop taking people's word for it.

151. Heaven is not my future. It's my everlasting place for eternity.

152. Preach against hell, not how powerful hell is.

153. Too many messages on who hates you. More messages on Blessed are you who have been persecuted for righteousness.

154. Preach me the mystery of the Kingdom of God. Hell is not the mystery of the Kingdom. It's the consequences for those who refuse the mystery of the Kingdom.

155. Jesus Christ is the hope of glory. That glory is eternal life in heaven in the Father's presence.

156. Just because you are different doesn't mean you

don't belong. It only means you are the revolutionary; you are the future.

157. Jesus can't love only those you love. He loves those you hate as well.

158. The gospel does not have prejudice in it. Jesus loves all.

159. A prophetic service is an appointment where God meets and speaks to His children.

160. Heaven will be more than you expected.

161. There's no shame in the gospel. It is the raw power of God.

162. Because of sin, certain animals can never look right in our eyes and dreams. But Noah and Adam had the privilege of coexisting.

163. Your best plan of success should be making it to heaven, to the Lord's house. Mark that on your busy daily calendar so you don't forget.

164. If the church leaders know how to forgive, the church members will do the same.

165. All Hail King Jesus! We proclaim His Majesty over all the earth.

BIBLICAL QUOTES AND LIFE QUOTES | 23

166. Jesus is not limited in any place. He can manifest Himself anywhere. All you have to do is call Him, and He will reach out His hands in hell and bring you out.

167. A lot of people in church still don't know how to pray. It's not fully their fault. Most church leaders don't pray because they don't know how to pray.

168. We live in the present life, sunup, and sundown. With God, it's the future.

169. God doesn't want your curiosity. He needs your attention.

170. The earth is without color without heaven.

171. Tomorrow is not promised. With faith in God, it is.

172. Humanity becomes sensitive and gets offended about anything because they know they are not right with God.

173. Connect to a prophet who hears God. Not a prophet that could hear your bank account.

174. Prophecy is not about how deep you went or how accurate you were. It's how helpful and truthful you were.

175. They are still waiting for you to fail. They are still holding meetings against you. They are still

prophesying falsehood against you. But if God is before you, who can be against you? Let them wait. Let them host meetings. Let them prophesy falsely. They shall come one way and flee seven ways.

176. Some are not seeking Jesus. They just want power without caring about the condition of their souls or eternity.

177. Don't waste the time of asking a prophet to prophesy on you when you don't believe in the prophetic ministry in the first place.

178. I'm convinced demons are viruses that attack the mind. You can get it through conversation, people, television, social media, etc. Anything that has to do with man-made things can give you that virus. It will destroy your mind and corrupt your heart. That will lead to possession.

179. Social media is one of the greatest threats to the church. Most have said it's a platform to preach the gospel. With so much disorder, social media causes people to go against God in the name of God. It destroys spiritual lives. Social media shows a fig tree with leaves but no fruit.

180. Those of you who are tired of church, who are tired of the bible, who are tired of revival, who are tired of listening to sermons, a time will come, when

you will get what you asked for—a big break. But then you will regret having ever asked for such a time as this. Run the race. Run even when you're so tired.

181. Pray while you can. Fast while you can. Worship while you can. A time is coming when you won't be able to.

182. Don't just try to hear God. Don't just try to know God. But build a relationship with God.

183. Never allow... God used to use me. God used to speak to me, or I used to feel his presence. Or I used to have deep dreams, or I used to read the Bible. I used to pray. I used to go to church. I used to sing. Don't be the used-to prophet, the used-to prophetess, the used-to preacher, or the used-to visionary. If you are in that league, you have left the presence of the Lord to do something on your own. And if you continue to do what you used to without a fresh revelation and a new wine, you are deceiving God's people. You need to get back on track. Be careful with the use of believers. They left His presence for their own carnality.

184. Offense is a sign of weakness, uncertainty, and insecurity.

185. Some people in the body have a big mouth but little action to show for it. Faith without deeds is dead.

186. The Kingdom of God is not a matter of talk but of power.

187. I will take the revelation of the word any day over philosophy. How can I walk away from the undeniable power of God for mere philosophy?

188. You can kill what God is raising, but you can't kill what He resurrected.

189. Where the spirit of poverty is, there will also be witchcraft. The church is against poverty, not with poverty.

190. If heaven is not real, then the earth is only a nightmare we need to wake up from.

191. When you start seeing heaven, you realize how much trouble the earth has had and that the only solution to it is from heaven.

192. God does not like to bless, set free, and heal people who don't know how to say Thank you.

193. FORGIVENESS IS A CURE... Learn to forgive, and learn to ask for forgiveness.

194. The great move of glory is about to begin. Position yourself. Heaven is so busy getting ready to pour down on earth.

195. Gentiles will inherit heaven as well. Bless the Father for Jesus Christ's making it possible.

196. The word of God will cause you to believe. But the power of God will get you to react—cause and effect.

197. Church people make everything that's against the church go viral. It's not worldly people; it's people that go to church. Cain said he was not his brother's keeper.

198. I'm not trying to be. I AM THAT I AM.

199. Fitting in with the crowd will bring you the people's favor. Letting God use you to make the difference will bring you God's fullness.

200. There's a coming glory, and it's called Glory Invasion.

201. Freedom is hard. That's why you should let the Holy Spirit lead.

202. People will hate you and don't know why they hate you. And they call it the Holy Spirit speaking to them. Stay focused. It's a distraction of the enemy.

203. You've got to allow Him to work in your life. You can be sad; that's okay. Just don't deny Him.

204. Whether you're weak or strong, no matter the situation, stay with the Lord.

205. Man can do what he wants, but the Lord can restore.

206. When you're in the will of God, you synchronize with all creation. Things just submit and obey.

207. God works better for you when you give Him time.

208. Prayer gets better with age and responsibilities.

209. We are agents of love, not abuse love and condemn people. Everyone deserves the love of God. For love covers a multitude of sins.

210. Christianity = Faith

211. There are true prophets. Don't look for them. Ask God to lead you to them.

212. You can't rush God's presence. How dare you? Churches today are so disrespectful to the presence of God. Moses didn't know he was going to spend 40 days on top of the mountain. Those that wait on the Lord…

213. Church, you have an assignment to bring people out of sin to righteousness. But rather, you are judging them for a debt that has been paid. But there is something that is coming that will be worse than sin. And we all need to prepare ourselves for the reign of the antichrist.

214. Christianity is the light of the world. Simply put, we don't need to be deep, blinding people's eyes... Just be a light for them so they can see.

215. You can't use the power of God if you don't understand his mercies. Not grace, not love, but mercy.

216. Truly, it is the season of giving.

217. The best place to find greatness is in the dump or trash. It's the rejected stone that becomes the capstone.

218. It will ruin your life to have a bitter heart.

219. Anyone who can deny themselves to see Jesus can be great.

220. The reason someone doesn't preach the gospel of grace and peace is because they are not fully delivered and free.

221. The Lord loves to pick up trash and turn it into treasure. Self-condemnation is a suicide pill.

222. Only the word of God can produce hunger in you for God.

223. The church doesn't unite people; the word of God does.

224. God doesn't use whoever He finds; He uses whoever He wants.

225. If you want someone to move into a neighborhood, you don't tell them about another neighborhood that is filled with trash. Advertise heaven, right?

226. A hell message will bring self-condemnation. A heavenly message will bring self-repentance.

227. You preach hell so much that it looks so big and is blocking them from seeing heaven.

228. Stop describing how horrible the hell is. That's not where you want them to go. You are scaring them. Job says, "What I fear happens to me." Tell them about heaven and how beautiful it is. It will attract more souls.

229. A heavenly message has more impact than a hellish message.

230. The Holy Spirit is not it. He is a person.

231. When dealing with men, God has a limit. He is limitless, but when it comes to men, He has a limit.

232. Many preachers are emotional. It's all noise. They hype your flesh, not your spirit. The soul won't change until your spirit is in control.

233. I would rather a preacher copy what their covering or spiritual father preaches than copy

something from someone you have no idea who they are.

234. Many preachers preach what they don't believe to keep a crowd and the money coming.

235. It's sad that many preachers don't believe in miracles, healing, prophecy, or the power of God.

236. It's sad that many preachers never read the whole bible.

237. It's sad that many preachers don't believe in the deliverance ministry.

238. It's sad that many preachers never had an encounter with The Lord.

239. It's sad that many preachers don't believe in heaven.

240. It cost God so much that he couldn't be among the human race; only a chosen people can he walk with. That's when his thirst for evangelism started… preaching the gospel to save souls.

241. Stop focusing on what you can do. Start focusing on what you were called to do.

242. Prayer is better when you don't want anything on earth.

243. Every time you entertain an angel of God, you please God, not humans, but angels. You are entertaining the wrong kind of people or beings.

244. In this generation, there's only one message that needs to be repeated over and over again. Stop pretending and be real. You can't fake it to make it. Pray for it, work for it, and serve until you make it.

245. I don't trust my conscience when it already knows. I don't trust my mind when it already knows. I don't trust what I already know. I don't know it, so I can learn it.

246. If the failures before didn't destroy you, the failures now won't either.

247. You have to be merciful. You need to have kindness. People who have kindness are strong people. You need to have humility. Humility helps your walk as a Christian. In the world, you needed pride because, in the world, God wasn't your protector. In the Kingdom of God, you need humility, meekness, and the ability to endure.

248. Prophecy is an invitation to do what God says. When you hear it, something has to be done about it.

249. Every time you say you love yourself, you need to do a self-check.

250. God can't give you big things with a mediocre mind.

251. So how do you know right from wrong? You don't. But you are learning them every day. At different ages and times, you are still learning them.

252. Whatever you think you know, you never learned it.

253. Most of the time, it is church people who make the prophetic look fake. Because of their abusive and controlling nature toward a prophet. They don't respect any spiritual laws.

254. The believer can't do without grace. You need daily grace. Every law is irrelevant when grace speaks. Grace breaks protocol.

255. Grace is the raw material for greatness in the Kingdom of God. Nothing can make you great except grace.

256. In life, you need only two people to make it. You need a friend, and you need an enemy. Had it not been for Goliath, David would not have been known.

257. Learn from someone better than you, and you will become a better version of yourself.

258. Were you comfortable with what you are now comfortable with before? Then, get uncomfortable so you can grow and learn new things.

259. Stop reflecting on yesterday for tomorrow.

260. Anything you are afraid of can happen again because you are afraid of it. It will bully you.

261. If working on you is not easy, it means you want to be bound. You don't want to live life.

262. You plan so much for yourself that it makes you unable to accept others without making a plan about it.

263. Asking is not begging. Someone who asks does so because they know what they need. Someone who begs does so because they know what they want. Someone who asks has a future. Someone who begs has only today.

264. You can only ask to learn how to fish. You beg for a piece of the fish. Those who ask are hard workers. Those who beg are lazy.

265. Someone who asks is full of humility. Someone who begs will beg with pride and arrogance.

266. A Man of God is nothing without Jesus. There are many gods. As well, no one goes to the Father but through Him.

267. If you don't make time for God, you are not investing in your future.

268. The heart was meant to love, not destroy or hate. That's why sickness or anxiety is controlling this generation. Learn to love.

269. Anyone who says Jesus is not real, don't take their word for it. Everyone, including them, will die one day. The truth will be confirmed for them.

270. Jesus is still on the throne. Keep faith in Him. He won't fail you.

271. Too many prophets died by their own kind… too many… too many.

272. As time advances, false prophets will get stronger. The true prophets will lay down their lives for the Kingdom.

273. It's easier to live when you're not looking for people's compliments.

274. Hypocrisy 101: People will call sin and judge whom they don't like, but the one they like, and God is working on them, leave them alone for the same thing they are judging someone else about.

275. Don't trust someone who hides their mistakes.

276. You don't need to explain to people what you already paid for. Show them the receipts.

277. Jesus is still on the throne. Goodness and mercy shall follow you all the days of your life.

278. Some people are balls of fire. You don't mess with them, or you will get burned.

279. Without submission, a whole generation could crash and send the next one to search.

280. Certain things you can't overcome don't mean giving up. Become strategic and wise about it until you can overcome it.

281. When something bad happens to you, you will know how many people really don't care for you. Not everyone is really celebrating you. Don't wait for their applause or for them to pat you on the back. Just keep moving.

282. Don't serve God out of fear. But out of love He has for you.

283. Be in tune with God's creations, yourself, and Jesus Christ. You seem tense and unbalanced; that's the root of frustration.

284. You get to see another day. Stop complaining and keep moving.

285. The same mouth that's cheering will one day turn against you. Don't focus on people cheering for you. They will say Hosanna and later crucify him. Focus on what you need to do. Don't mind the cheerleader.

286. The person who's righteous to you had to hurt a lot of people to get to that level. Nobody is perfect.

287. Money can't buy everything. It can never buy your eternity.

288. You don't see them or hear from them because they are not trying to be there for your success. They want to be there at your funeral. That's why you should not worry about them. Keep moving and celebrate yourself.

289. Prophecy is not for entertainment. It's speaking the mind of God.

290. The secret place is not a public place.

291. The last minute is on time for God. You saw it at the last minute, but it's the right time for God.

292. We are not the only existing beings in the universe. We are just the most stubborn and independent beings in the universe. But yet, He gave us a chance to do things right.

293. The person you hate is your greatest inspiration and motivation. Be careful who you hate. You might be competing in the wrong race. Well, hate the devil. He will inspire you and motivate you to be righteous.

294. God is getting ready to bless everyone who believes and is ready to walk with Him. You don't need to lie or deceive people for money or what you need. Or He will expose you.

295. Your faith has to be contagious when it's real.

296. People can quickly become addicted to preaching but not to prayer. Destructive: preaching without prayer is powerless.

297. You're a winner. Not be a winner. You are a winner.

298. Don't ever let your enemies matter more to you than the people who care for and love you.

299. Many are getting impatient; they can't wait for you to fail. For someone with a vision, failure is part of the journey. If we say we're not going to fail, we condemn ourselves to fail and never recover from it.

300. Where there's no prophecy, people run wild and have no restraint. Because there are no prophets to reveal the mind of God to them and the power of

prophecy. As much as you don't like prophets, He gave some to be prophets.

301. Christianity does not define who we are. The word of God and sound doctrine do.

302. What makes humans so powerful is living in contradiction to themselves and each other. We are destructive to each other, even when we love each other.

303. I heard them say that there is no salvation in Christianity. Of course, they are right... Everyone is a Christian these days. But there is salvation in Jesus. Just because someone is a Christian doesn't mean they are saved.

304. We live in a generation where parents are trying to outlive their own kids. That's why Jesus cannot return yet. The order has been disrupted everywhere.

305. If they want you to believe in the ancestors, that's fine. Who did the ancestors believe in?

306. If you don't believe in Jesus, don't even think about believing in God.

307. You don't believe in God when everything else fails you, and you believe in them. Will you believe in God now? The doctors won't die with you. Science doesn't know if there is life after death. The medicine

won't cure you. Will you believe in God if everything you believe in fails you?

308. No one's life is better than another's. We might not go through it at the same time or in the same way, but we go through it. At some point, you begin to have questions that science cannot answer. Only God can answer them.

309. As much as living is great, we will all die someday. We all have a time to die, and we don't know the time. Are you prepared for what is next after death?

310. In life, there will always be a resolution. Just make sure you do it in the right way.

311. In this world, our time here is limited. But you have time to fulfill your dreams and vision. Only God's hand can work it like that.

312. This generation is trying to be funny so much that they forget or don't know how to be serious about anything.

313. Being a member of one church and staying there and not hopping and leaving is a blessing for that person. Of course, it must be a church led by the Holy Spirit. The growth of that person is in the church they are a member of. Not only spiritual growth, but every area of growth.

314. There's power in prayer.

315. In this generation, success doesn't make you popular. Fail, and you will see how many people know you. Most of your followers are not following you because you're succeeding. They can't wait for you to fail because of the way you are going, so they're following you while they wait. THE SAME MOUTH THAT SAID HOSANNA IS THE SAME MOUTH THAT WILL SAY CRUCIFY HIM.

316. Why do you pray if you're not looking for results?

317. The way the world is, you must always pray to never be at the wrong place at the wrong time.

318. THERE'S A COMING GLORY FROM THE THRONE OF GOD... IT WILL BE A GLORY INVASION!

319. Someone who is afraid to tell people the truth is someone who doesn't like to hear the truth. Anything built on a lie will not stand.

320. To succeed... 1 does not equal 1. A couple of things equal 1... It takes a band to make music, but it's one song. It takes more than two to make a family, but it's one family.

321. God does answer prayers.

322. There are true prophets all over... (7000 that have not bowed to false gods), believe it or not.

323. In this world, peace is a time to prepare and strengthen yourself for the next conflict. Every time you miss your rest stop, you set yourself up to get overwhelmed.

324. Don't trust anyone who's leading who doesn't have a broken hip.

325. It's not the Man of God that's powerful. It was the people who were sent to him that made the anointing flow easier or the people he was sent to.

326. If it doesn't work, try again as much as you can until it does. Just don't give up!

327. I can, I used to, and I will continue to. – GOD

328. Give Jesus everything, and He will transform everything.

329. Church people will ask God to send help, and when the help comes, they will use it and kill it afterward.

330. Finding someone to talk to about God's word is difficult these days; to share revelations in the scriptures. Iron sharpens iron.

331. The contest between God's goodness and tribulations is a draw. Without tribulations, you will never understand God's goodness. So, if you feel like giving up because it's too hard for you, you will miss God's goodness.

332. Just that easy, if we could have seen what God has for us—the rooms Jesus has prepared for us—the kind of life in eternity. If we could have seen it like the rich man saw Lazarus in Abraham's bosom, suicide would have become a way to travel. Don't miss out on what God has prepared for you. Jesus IS THE ONLY WAY!

333. You can't preach to people if you don't love them.

334. Prophets like to scatter seeds of the prophetic, even if they take years to grow. Eventually, you will see it. THUS SAITH THE LORD OF HOST: GET YOURSELF READY FOR THE FULFILLMENT OF HIS WORD.

335. When your God-appointed time has come, you don't wish anymore. You don't hope... You don't feel lucky anymore. You just know this is it. Your life has changed forever. I prophesy on you. Your time has come.

336. Apostle Paul... 1 Corinthians 14:31 For you can all prophesy one by one that all may learn and all may

be encouraged. We would not have needed technology if every Christian was prophetic.

337. It's a prayer that fulfills prophecy. Not information.

338. Church people don't like when God is using you. They only rejoice when you fall. They don't trust you when God is using you. But they will work with agents of the devil.

339. If you believe in God's prophets, even the little things they say to you, don't take it lightly. Watch and pray about it. You don't want to regret it later on.

340. Stay connected to the no-name because God is about to give a name (the name reveal season is coming). He was known as a dream interpreter in jail and a dreamer at his father's house. Until God says he is Joseph, ruler of Egypt and the world.

341. Your flesh is not the church. Stop saying we are the church. He said I will build my church. He didn't build the church from flesh or from you. He builds the church by His Spirit. The Holy Spirit. If you don't have the spirit of Christ in you, you can't be the church. The Holy Spirit is the one who helps with that. That is why we gather in His name because we boost each other up and kill the flesh. So, the spirit who raised Him from the

dead could dwell in us. The church is made up of those with the spirit of Christ, not the flesh. When we received Him, we decided to kill the flesh and live for Him.

342. It will be proven that the church is the answer to all the questions and issues that are going on around the world. People say we are the church. The flesh is not the church. It's not the flesh. He seeks true worshippers who will worship Him in spirit and in truth. It's the spirit of Him in you that makes the church. Other than that, it's a synagogue of Satan. The church is the answer. God will prove it.

343. THE ANOINTING TAKES TIME.

344. The anti-Christ will be a religious man. A man of great spirituality and insight. Not a politician but will rule politicians because of spiritual powers. He will know the Bible, and he will declare himself to be god, and that the God of the Bible is false.

345. In times of crisis, unnecessary spending is demonic. Sowing seeds and offering are investments in crisis. Surely it will bring a harvest.

346. When you finally win all the battles that have been against and all around you and prosperity and greatness are kicking in, Satan will use his greatest weapon against you. Yourself against yourself... WIN.

347. Wisdom is gold. In seasons like this, everything counts. Be wise in all that you do.

348. Wealth will change hands. Position yourself. Position yourself.

349. Never force your vision on someone who has not been called to be part of it.

350. The world is very opinionated about everything, to the point where they are lost in their own opinions. That's why we preach the gospel. The word of God is not opinion. It's the truth.

351. If there's no prophet in a town, then there's no growth, no business plans, and no economy. The next generation will suffer—no fear of God, no harvest.

352. Through a prophet, the Lord brought Israel out of Egypt, and through a prophet, he was guarded.

353. It's better to be a servant in God's house than a master in the devil's work.

354. When we have faith in God, things don't magically happen. He grants wisdom, understanding, knowledge, and power to deal with what you are facing. You become a superhuman.

355. You may all prophesy... but you are not all prophets.

356. Prophets who prophesy to gain people's favor are hypocrites. A lying spirit was sent to their tongues.

357. Prophets who use the prophetic to trick young prophets are dangerous. They are the old (rejected) prophets.

358. Prophets who prophesy on someone and when it comes to pass, they feel a certain way and start fighting the person they prophesied the word of the Lord to are suspects…Balaam prophets.

359. There is hope. God is in control.

360. When everything else does not work, people ask, Why don't the prophets prophesy? If you weren't listening before, will you be able to listen now? Because God will not say it the way you want, it will still be His way.

361. You are as guilty as the person you judge. Jesus just got to you before he got to them. Why don't you help them get to know Him (Jesus) so they can receive grace as well? Selfish generation… Share the gospel, not your version of the gospel.

362. It's more exciting to talk about Jesus than to prophesy. Most of the time, it's talking about Jesus that leads to prophesying.

363. Eighty percent of the church doesn't help people; they bully people to show they are not sinners like them. How will that save your soul?

364. God is a generational God. You can always trace Him back to the beginning if you become part of the generation, HE ESTABLISHED. HE IS REAL…

365. God doesn't have a problem with you living life to the fullest. He has a problem that you don't acknowledge and give credit to Him and your older brother His Son.

366. Maturity plays a big role in being anointed.

367. It's not every opportunity that gives you opportunities. Some opportunities actually spell disappointment. Spells are different, and sound different, but are the same word. Wisdom is not a spelling error.

368. True prophets don't want to be seen or heard but are happy to speak the word of the Lord—nothing more than that. But, in confidence in the spirit power, they knew they heard from God revealing the mind of God to His people.

369. Church problems today… They want to be known and are not letting people know Jesus.

370. The fight in this world is between evil and good, not between evil and God.

371. You don't pray for money to come. You pray for God to give you skills so money can come.

372. Money is not attracted by prayers. Money is attracted by the work of your hands. Your gift will make room for you.

373. A tree that doesn't bow to the wind, will be destroyed by the storm.

374. True prophets prophesy for nothing in return. Naaman, gold means nothing.

375. A prophet is without honor in his own home.

376. It's a good thing to be used by God, but It's everything to have a relationship with Him.

377. Be careful what you get yourself into too deep about. It may look like nothing, but going too deep means you're comfortable. Getting out will be difficult. Get too deep into being a believer in Christ.

378. Anyone who doesn't trust themselves cannot prophesy or be a prophet.

379. The closer we get to the coming of the Lord, death will make more sense—at least for Christians.

380. The fear of the Lord will spread on the earth once more. Watch and pray.

381. Last time I checked, it was the church that was sending people to hell; it wasn't God. Jesus never commands the church to send people to hell. He said to preach to them to be saved, not preach to them they're going to hell. Hell is not salvation; Jesus is.

382. If the church helped unbelievers more than preached and condemned believers, the Lord would have saved more people. The church is not a cult.

383. We need our faith to meet our dimensions. We need our faith to increase with our levels.

384. When it comes to the case of faith, no impartation, no anointing, and no power could build your faith.

385. The more I can hear the word, the more faith I can build in myself.

386. Jesus did not use the mustard seed because it was smaller. He used it because it grew bigger.

387. The body of Christ is not wealthy, not because God doesn't answer prayer but because we are selfish. Every single Christian is supposed to be prospering.

388. Without hearing from God, we become lost. Without hearing from God, we become destructive. Without hearing from God, we become violent.

389. They deny the existence of God but look for another God. They replace him with the sun, the moon, or creation itself. They replace God with human beings and begin to worship human beings.

390. Whatever else replaces God will fail you. The person you trust so much will fail you. The job you love so much will fail you. Because God is irreplaceable. No one can fill that position. No one can replace God.

391. It was God who made it happen. The moment you replace him, Satan has power over your life. Your life will be upside down.

392. How do I hear His (God's) voice? It's not a voice; it's a relationship. You don't hear a voice; you have a relationship.

393. It's a life that dies that brings life. A life must die so that another life may live. It's a life that gives life. A life for a life.

394. Someone who denies Jesus Christ as the Son of God is an antichrist. If you can't accept the death and resurrection of Jesus Christ, you cannot have life. His life becomes yours because he died for you. When you

reject that sacrifice, you reject healing, deliverance, provision, and power.

395. The power is in the blood. Life is in the blood.

396. When you accept Jesus, you give him your soul, "the blood."

397. Satan cannot kill your spirit. A spirit cannot die. Satan can only attack your soul to destroy you. If he attacks your soul, it is over for you. Only God can bring you out. The minute you accept Jesus, he becomes your soul.

398. You can't go into the future to repent. You have to turn back. The moment you accept the sacrifice of Jesus, repentance comes in.

399. If you can accept that sacrifice today, there is no problem in you that doesn't have a solution. Recognize that Jesus died for you, and his life becomes yours.

400. The devil can't kill what's already dead.

401. There's no sin he didn't die for. When you call a Christian a sinner, it disrespects the sacrifice. We were sinners who are now righteous.

402. Accept Christ as your Lord and Savior, and his holiness becomes your holiness. No one can work for

holiness. No one can work for righteousness. That's why Jesus died.

403. What we call sin is really a demon. You can cast out demons.

404. The church is where all the problems are supposed to be. The church is a hospital.

405. God had to become man to save man because God gave man the world.

406. We are telling people that God can do it when He already did it.

407. The power of God is in the message that God preaches.

408. The only power in preaching is when you're preaching about the cross.

409. Jesus left the tomb. With the fact that he left the tomb, there is a power that is made available to us. An empty tomb means deliverance. An empty tomb means miracles. An empty tomb means a breakthrough.

410. Even if you don't believe that you can see Jesus, if you believe that the tomb is empty, you can get miracles.

411. The presence of God is everywhere. The manifest

presence of God only comes when people know how to worship.

412. It's not prayer that heals the sick. It's the relationship you have with God that will heal the sick.

413. Do you know why the devil doesn't like you? Because God lives in you. Do you know why the devil doesn't like you? Because he's already judged. He doesn't have a place in heaven anymore. He's lost his place. But you have a chance.

414. You have authority, you have power, and you have dominion.

415. Your blessing is hidden in your shout. If you only say it in your heart, you aren't going to shake the devil. You've got to be aggressive and shout. Tell the devil, "Enough is enough; it's my time to come out to shine."

416. There's power in your words and in your actions. There's power on the inside of you.

417. Where faith is lacking, God becomes bigger.

418. Don't let people disqualify you when God has already qualified you.

419. God does not trust us enough to worship Him. That is why He gave us the Holy Ghost. That is why we must worship Him in spirit and in truth.

420. You need to find out what curses are in your family and deal with them in the name of Jesus.

421. You speak too much negativity; speak good things.

422. The devil doesn't decide your life; your family doesn't decide your life. It's your mouth's decision.

423. Speak good things over your life. As you speak, you will shape your destiny.

424. Bondage is what destroys the good things God made available in your life.

425. Every time we make a few steps forward, bondage pushes us 10 steps backward.

426. When you are in bondage, your gift is still used, but it is the enemy that is using your gift.

427. You can feel the power, but if you don't have the word, you can't keep the power. Because of the word, the power stays. It's because of the word that power flows.

428. Just because you believe does not mean you know the truth. You can believe, but you don't know the truth.

429. The truth will set you free. You cannot say that God can heal you. The truth is that He will heal you.

You cannot say that God can deliver you. The truth is that He will deliver you.

430. The only one who can set you free is Jesus. Even if you know Jesus, if you don't know his word, you will not be set free. When you hear his word and receive the truth, then the truth will set you free.

431. When you know the truth, the truth shall make you free. When you know the truth, it's going to break your bond.

432. God can do it for you; all you have to do is hear the word.

433. You have to remind yourself of the truth of the word of God.

434. The moment you're reminded of the truth of God, then you begin to feel the power. You begin to feel strength. You begin to feel like you can do it. You begin to feel like no blockage can stop you. Why? Because the truth is in you.

435. What does a cross mean? "As a sign of death—or an intersection of God's love and justice—you must walk in death.

436. If you don't know the cross, then you don't know life.

437. Only when I'm alone can I hear the Lord. God doesn't talk to you when everyone is around you.

438. He didn't call us when we were righteous. It was while we were sinners that He called us out.

439. Being born again is not cleaning your outside. It's cleansing your insides.

440. The spirit of tradition hinders people from receiving God's glory.

441. The absence of righteousness is destruction!

442. The first act of Christianity was an Ark. Everyone who is a Christian today is in an Ark.

443. Noah represents Jesus. His family represents Israel. The animals represent pagans. The Ark represents the salvation of God.

444. Jesus is the reincarnation of God. If you reject Jesus, you reject God. Not because Jesus is following God. But because he is God.

445. If your soul rejects Christ, your soul rejects life; your soul rejects healing; your soul rejects deliverance.

446. The moment you stop seeing Christ, miracles and healing pass by.

447. God did not speak the law. He spoke the law through Moses. The laws of God will kill you. He had to come down to your level to speak laws at your level.

448. There are two people in the bible who never lost a fight. That is David and Jesus.

449. The life of Moses reflects the life of Jesus Christ.

450. The bosom you are supposed to rest on is a father's bosom, not a stranger's.

451. Everything you do on this earth; you must plant a seed.

452. Only someone who has been with Jesus can give you Jesus.

453. The beginning of everything always looks good, but the beginning of the earth is chaotic. Where there is no law, there is no God.

454. Since Jesus walked this earth, it has been a constant present. The blood still has the same value.

455. The reason we can't discern what is coming tomorrow is because tomorrow is still today and yesterday is still tomorrow.

456. This is how God works: He releases the revelation in the spirit. Whoever is connected will take it.

457. We're not supposed to be telling people they're going to hell. We're supposed to be telling people they're going to be delivered from hell.

458. Satan had access to do whatever he wanted, but the Lord took it back.

459. There's no time to rest when Satan is fighting.

460. Death is a punishment for disobedience.

461. Time is power. Time is not money. There is no money that can pay for your time. No amount of money can buy your time. If there is a price on your time, then it is of no value to destiny.

462. God made everything in season. If God created things in time, then He's on the same level as you are. It is impossible for God to function within time.

463. If you are made of words, God is made of revelations and mysteries.

464. You are the revelation of God and the mystery of God. Everything that is created is a revelation and mystery of God.

465. Not everyone can build in the anointing. Some of you need a covering to draw from.

466. There is a thin line between anointing and

emotions. You might not be anointed; you might be emotional.

467. Jesus is still on the throne… Goodness and mercy shall follow you all the days of your life.

468. Rebellion is opposition to authority. Rebellion doesn't start in your mind; it starts in your heart.

469. Anyone who is in rebellion and is independent is selfish and self-centered.

470. Do you know the divine authority that God has set? If I cannot submit to authority, automatically, rebellion has seized me.

471. When a man fights with you, God can intervene. But what about when God fights with you, who can help you? That is why you must submit to the divine authority of God.

472. Rebellion doesn't give you time to think. Rebellion looks and reacts.

473. The absence of discipline is the absence of obedience. Anyone who doesn't have any standards is not disciplined.

474. The gospel of Jesus Christ is not competition.

475. The Anointing of the Holy Spirit is not for sale. So don't bribe a Man of God because of anointing.

And don't think because you are anointed, you can do whatever you want. The anointing is not for sale.

476. There is no easy way out of the plan of God. The Bible says many are called, but few are chosen. If everything is easy for you, then you are still called. Because when you are chosen, there is no easy way out of it but to be persecuted, through trials and tribulations. Don't look for an easy way out of the plan of God for your life. Endure hardships.

477. He who believes in God will never be disappointed. Men can disappoint you or fail you. God will never fail you or disappoint you.

478. Only human disappointments can make one rely on, trust, and believe in God's guidance. If you had never gone through what you have been through, you would have never trusted, relied on, and believed God so much.

479. Whenever your eyes lose focus on who has chosen you, disappointments will be your PhD. Keep your eyes focused on Jesus.

480. Flesh and blood want you to walk in its image; meaning the image of tradition, religion cursed, etc. But you must resist and submit yourself to Christ's image, which is Resurrection and Life.

481. Faith without belief is doubt. Belief without faith is doubt.

482. In order to have true faith in God, you must truly believe in his servant.

483. Disobedience got the world in trouble. Obedience will get it out of trouble.

484. The rest of God is what will give you the ability to walk right as a Christian.

485. The rest of God gives you peace, but not as the world understands.

486. When you become a Christian, your attitude has to change because you're not in survival mode anymore.

487. To get the rest of God, you have to change the way you think.

488. Zoeway: a genial life. A life active and devoted to God. Walk in the footsteps of Jesus. When you have the zoeway, supernatural things start to happen.

489. Real prayer is not asking God for anything. It is asking God for Himself.

490. As a Christian, there are limitations. We can't live the way the world lives.

491. When the wicked bend their bow, you must stand on the Rock.

492. Some people say women should not preach the gospel. It was a woman who carried the word of God.

493. Never argue the word of God.

494. You don't receive God in your mind. You receive Him in your heart.

495. The wicked person shoots you in one place, your heart.

496. Those with a pure heart shall see God. A pure heart means you don't keep anything in there but the love of God.

497. A church is not a church until it looks like its Pastor. If you don't care, you hurt the Pastor. The Pastor has an account to give. You have to follow…look like your leader.

498. Prophetic ministry comes with rebuke. It's different from a pastoral ministry.

499. If you are fighting against the prophetic anointing, you are destroying your own self. You have an account. Don't just do what you feel like doing.

500. Time is an altar of sacrifice.

501. Not knowing or understanding what God reveals to you will attract demonic entities.

502. If you don't understand angels, you can't understand God's message or revelation.

503. You're supposed to be a life-giving spirit, not a living being.

504. Anything without a foundation will fall quickly.

505. Fasting doesn't give you power, it gives you clarity.

506. Earth cannot function without heaven. Heaven cannot function without earth. In order for heaven to release, there needs to be an earth to receive.

507. When God gives a dream or vision, it does not come from above. Every vision or dream is tied to your surroundings.

508. The Holy Spirit can give you a dream. Your emotions can give you a dream. Satan can give you a dream.

509. The answer to a dream doesn't come from within, it comes from above.

510. Mystery is all over the earth and heaven. The mystery is God Himself.

511. If you catch a mystery, the answer to that mystery has to come from above.

512. Satan was never your enemy. He is God's enemy, not ours. Satan is the opposite of Jesus.

513. An angel is a revelation of the mystery. The fallen angel is the seed of Satan. They are revelations from you outside of God's presence.

514. The more I read, the more it will inspire me to see what I need to see.

515. Remembering is a type of vision.

516. Your demons are more powerful than Satan.

517. One thing about Jesus… He looks for the leftovers. He looks for what they left to die. He looks for the rejected stones. And He turns them into somebody. Whose report will you believe?

518. God's judgment is not your hatred and how you feel about other people. It is just and righteous. Everyone has a portion.

519. In the scriptures, Jesus gets so excited when he sees people's faith… not gifts… not talents… not what you can do. But now all you see is dead works. There's no excitement in people because there is no faith. Faith makes things… more wonders and miracles.

520. To build treasures you must have obedience, faith in God, and walk by the Holy Spirit.

521. You must deny yourself to follow a Man of God.

522. Talents and gifts don't change lives. The Bible says your gift will make room for you. Just because you're gifted doesn't mean you're ready.

523. If you don't get the teachings, you're not a disciple, you're a deceiver. It's in the teaching that will allow the anointing to keep flowing.

524. To follow the Man of God, doesn't mean you are following a man.

525. You won't find a prophet. The prophet finds you. It's God who makes the connection.

526. Honor means what is taught to you, you become. Picking up the character and succeeding.

527. Christianity is not a religion. It's a nationality.

528. The earth is not functional without heavenly grace.

529. God's will is not done on earth. God's will is done in heaven and then reflected on earth.

530. When you are connected to heaven, you don't look at things like everyone else. Your language is

different. Just speak the word and heaven will give it to you.

531. When you possess heaven, it's a revelation you receive. That revelation gives you access to things you never owned.

532. When you don't pray, you don't connect to heaven.

533. A Christian does not need to pray to ask God for anything. The more you are connected to Him, He just gives you.

534. The riches of God is not how much you save. It is how much He provides for you every day.

535. Wherever heaven and earth touch, God's presence is there.

536. God does not have a form. A man has to give Him form.

537. The power of when you know someone is praying for you…Jesus prayed for his disciples. He needed prayer too, but his disciples fell asleep because water can't pour upwards.

538. You cannot convince somebody to do something unless you do it yourself.

539. If you're overthinking, you will miss God.

540. The only way to see yourself is through the eyes of other people.

541. People who hate something they don't know or understand will always miss what they hate when it's gone. People who love what they understand or know will always remember what they love when it's gone.

542. Anything you are still holding on to isn't the past; it's the present.

543. Have faith until they see you weren't all talk... it's real!

544. Set yourself free from the past tense and become a prisoner of the future.

545. If it acts like a witch, it's a witch. If she talks like Jezebel, then she's Jezebel. If it quacks like a duck, then it's a duck.

546. One of the reasons you can't prosper... you love money, not what you are skilled to do... so you prostitute.

547. Getting angry, upset, panicked, etc. will make the situation worse.

548. There are legal actions. There are lawyers (advisors, Men of God, spiritual fathers, etc.) who can help you with legal action.

549. An accident is not planned. It just happens no matter how careful you are. In the same way, don't expect that what people do to you is something that's planned. No, they're not. But there are legal ways to deal with it.

550. The past is not to live in, but it is a school to learn from.

551. Always keep love as your defense. Guard your heart with love.

552. A strong person is someone who does the best they can to fix their mistakes... not run from them.

553. There's nothing that hurts them more... someone who's trying to hurt someone who never did anything to them to begin with. Be still and silent if you did nothing wrong. It will hurt them, not you.

554. Wisdom over skills.

555. Don't live because you are trying not to die. But live before you die. The earth is the Lord's and the fulness thereof.

556. Anyone who has access has a key to open doors.

557. On the road to greatness, everyone has to catch or hitch a ride.

558. Don't speak against someone because one day you might end up in the same situation. We are agents of love.

559. Sometimes success comes from people who hate you, not people who love you.

560. Be careful with people who use your pain as an advantage over you to fulfill their own goals but never help you heal.

561. I needed to be broke so I could learn how to budget.

562. I needed to work jobs that I hated so I could work hard to do what I love.

563. I needed to be laughed at when I told people about my dreams so I could turn them into my reality.

564. I needed to be separated from people so I could help lead them to greatness.

565. Every test, every trial, every door that closed, it was all worth it.

566. Preparation is a necessity of life.

567. Giving is easy. To receive could cost you your dignity.

568. There are some who will smile with you but inside kill you.

569. Anyone who follows will eventually lead. Anyone who is leading will eventually have to follow.

570. Whatever you learn while following someone, you have to lead someone else. In order to lead correctly, I have to follow someone else correctly.

571. If the love you say you have given up, then it was never love... It was perseverance.

572. When you know what you want, you will know what to give up.

573. You are more capable than you think. You just don't know your own strength and capabilities.

574. Don't have a big mouth with little action. Faith without works is dead.

575. It takes years to make fine wine. It will take years for people to see your greatness even after you're long gone. Don't give up... your reward is in Heaven.

576. Summertime is when the devil destroys finances. Be wise with your money this summer. Manage your movements as well because it is also the time many accidents happen.

577. Highlights are not the same as the game. The highlight looks good, but the game was tough. Don't judge someone based on highlights. You don't know their struggles to get where they are now.

578. If someone is scared of making mistakes because they believe they will look like a failure... that person is already a failure because they will always do everything backward from what will embarrass them or label them.

579. In hard labor and sweat, the Bible says we will harvest the ground.

580. We were cursed to work hard and learn things on our own through failure.

581. Mistakes are not a curse. They're the way of life to grow.

582. The harvest is plentiful... no need to compete or fight... It's plenty.

583. Some people don't speak like they write. Be careful what you're reading on Facebook. You may be following a devil that copies and pastes.

584. Your possessions, your job, your families, your businesses, they can wait. You're in need of God more than anything.

585. You don't win by winning. You win because you lost. It's only failure that can make you successful.

586. Would you ever go to a restaurant on a full stomach? Especially your favorite restaurant?

587. There are some who will take everything from you but never care for you.

588. Time is not money, it's power.

589. What is the order of what you want for your life?

590. A bold person is an empty shell noise maker... nothing to back up what they say.

591. A humble person is filled inside but outside is rough. They don't look like what they are saying.

592. If you feel what they are doing is wrong, do better. If you can't do better, keep your mouth shut.

593. Speak about what you can do to help people. Don't hate what others are doing to help people.

594. Everybody needs a voice of reason in their life. Don't look for a yes person.

595. The foundation of success is from the pain you've endured. You have to endure some things, so people know you are successful.

596. Maturity is to accept what's important.

597. Quitters are never remembered. The one who endures till the end creates a legacy. Truth is... Stop quitting on yourself!

598. Don't ever let your emotions confuse you to be like everyone else.

599. The more they are trying to stop you, the more strategic you will become. It's that simple.

600. The more people deny and reject you, the more courageous you will become. It's that simple.

601. The more you suffer, the wiser you become. It's that simple.

602. The more you struggle, the stronger you will become. It's that simple.

603. On the journey to success, you have to hitch a ride.

604. Just because you have a peeping game, don't call it discernment. It's just gossip.

605. The most dangerous person is someone who can't see themselves.

606. Everything is the same everywhere. Nothing is new under the sun. But everything in you can make everything everywhere different or new. Don't change

your environment. Change you and your environment will change.

607. They say you will fail. But on God's calendar, it says, "I know the plans I have for you. NOT TO FAIL. BUT TO SUCCEED." Let them talk; you will succeed.

608. Every beginning starts with criticism. But your finishing can come with standing ovations. Run the race and finish strong. The season for people to celebrate you is coming.

609. If you don't speak into the year about what you need to happen, the enemy will speak into the year to control your life. Every day you wake up, command the day, and let the wicked be shaken out of it.

610. Dirty people don't take showers. It's the people who want to stay clean that take showers. We all fall short. Remain clean. Don't be dirty.

611. If you stay long enough in the dark, it becomes visible. That doesn't mean it's light.

612. You don't even know how to win yourself. Don't even think about defeating the enemy.

613. Something to think about… while you are jealous of someone else, the whole time you are gifted in your own way.

614. Someone who seeks opportunities needs no gift. They need donations.

615. Never despise humility. It makes you weak, and that's why God is strong.

616. If you can listen and obey the voice that tells you to love your enemies, forgive those who wrong you, love those who hate you, walk in humility, keep your life clean, walk in sanctification and holiness, don't gossip, etc. If you can listen to that voice and obey it... you will understand the voice of God.

617. A ground that cannot be produced is not good for a man with seeds.

618. At times it's not a demon... you just have to **RESET, RESTART, RECONNECT.**

619. People who have a future don't have time to talk or gossip about people. If you have a future, let them talk and you keep working.

620. Your turn is special.

621. The moment your heart has faith, even though your mind disagrees, your heart will lead you.

622. You can only betray what you have no power to deal with out of a wicked heart.

623. The reason some gossip is that they are too lazy to achieve what others achieve.

624. The reason you don't forgive is because you know what you are capable of doing.

625. You can only be jealous of what doesn't belong to you.

626. Be careful when you hate. You could become what you hate.

627. The harder it is, the bigger the blessing will be. Just that simple.

628. The more they leave you alone, the more focused you will become. Just that simple.

629. The more people fail you and betray you, the less toxic your environment should become.

630. The more they are trying to kill you or destroy you, the more discerning you will become.

631. Not everyone can help you win. Not everyone can make you a champion, no matter how good you are. If you want to win, don't find winners, find people who can help you win.

632. The secret to living a life without cancer, high blood pressure, diabetes, and many other illnesses… or I could say the secret to not dying prematurely through

sickness… LOVE EVERYONE AND LIVE HAPPILY.

633. Money doesn't grow on trees, but it grows on how hard you work.

634. Success has a price. You will hurt some people. No matter how wise you are, you will hurt people.

635. What's worse than death is living without a purpose… running around like wild animals.

636. You can judge what is around you so much to the point, that your own judgment becomes a hindrance to your success. What you were lacking in education to understand, now you are educated to understand but you judge it. Now your pride won't allow you to be wrong and apologize. Be careful what and who you judge.

637. So many are waiting for you to fail. It's okay, don't wish wrong for them. Succeed so you can help them.

638. Some things no one can know about you but you. You don't need someone's approval but a confirmation. Many people who approved or disapproved of you were supposed to confirm you. Only you could know. You only need confirmation.

639. Many people are waiting for you to fail. They thought it was a bad thing. For a person with a dream

and vision, WITHOUT FAILURE, THERE IS NO SUCCESS.

640. The sign of faith...you don't know what is coming, but you still continue to build.

641. There are certain things in life that, if you're afraid of doing them because of a lack of money, will close your mind and make you believe that there's not enough money in the world. You will never know who has money until you start spending money.

642. Living a fast life is messing up loyalty and commitment in this generation.

643. There are some things God shares with you that are meant to be kept as a secret. Stop sharing openly... that's why you are not prospering.

644. It's not about who is rich and who has money. You don't want to be a beggar. But there's a level you want to reach in life, and there are some gifted and talented people you have to connect with. You have to know them. Don't be a beggar looking for the rich. Look for the gifted and talented. The rich connect with gifted and talented people.

645. Anyone you sow money into means you trust them with your destiny.

646. Stop asking God for money. Position yourself for it.

647. According to your faith, if you know someone is a true prophet of God, never go to them empty-handed. False prophets may abuse you, but you abuse true prophets.

648. A curse is a supernatural force that works to bring destruction to someone.

649. If you mind your own business, you don't have to worry about a curse.

650. You can't put yourself in places that will destroy you.

651. Anything you are tied up to in this world, the enemy can use it to destroy you.

652. Church is not a tradition; it's a lifestyle!

653. To receive from God, you have to be yourself.

654. People fight or defend themselves because they don't have confidence.

655. The more you talk, the more you expose yourself.

656. Someone with many excuses has no self-confidence. The reason you give excuses is that your

mind is racing against what you're hearing, and you don't know how to answer it, so you give excuses.

657. Someone with many excuses has no sense of responsibility. The devil can use that against you due to you not being confident.

658. Someone who is afraid of making mistakes has no self-confidence. You're afraid of making mistakes because you don't trust yourself.

659. If you don't believe in yourself, no one can believe in you. You have to get it wrong before you get it right.

660. Someone who is afraid of making mistakes has 1000% pride. When they do make mistakes, they will take it out on everyone.

661. Your greatest battle is your mind. Your mind has security systems!

662. Behind every stress and depression, there is sickness.

663. When someone loses their purpose and has nothing to live for, they are like savages.

664. Without the essence of God, we are like animals. Because when we have Him, He transforms our hearts, and that transformation makes us more than animals.

665. When we receive the promises of God, then we will have a sense of life.

666. If you don't have the promise of God in your life, then you are lost.

667. Most problems in the church are not problems. They are just revelations. It's only animals that try to pick a fight.

668. A promise is not for everyone to understand. It becomes a promise because not everyone understands it.

669. Anything in this world that promotes you can bring you down. But when Jesus promotes you, no one can bring you down.

670. What is your greatest fear? Face it, and you will be free.

671. Your past makes you stronger. Don't put it on you or hold onto it as your burden. Your past is not your burden.

672. Don't ever hide who you are because it will turn you into what you should be and should become. Who are you? Born sinners. What should you be or become? Sanctified folks. Your nature of sin brings out your holiness. In one word, "salvation" or "soteria," which means to be delivered, to be saved.

673. Emotions are a hindrance in your life, preventing you from feeling or hearing the voice of the Holy Spirit. Don't let your emotions deceive you.

674. If you don't stand for something, you will fall for anything. Refuse to be confused.

675. Commitment is the principle of discipline. The more committed you are, the more discipline you will have. Commitment is what you call the survival code. Be committed to the work of God, to your church, to serving. You will survive, and you will have discipline. This is the mind of God.

676. Commitment will break you down, changing your nature, and your personality, bringing about changes. Commitment will change the way you see and the way others see you. Commitment will make you a person of vision, a millionaire, an entrepreneur, a wealthy individual, and someone of character and prosperity. Commitment can make anything small become big. Commitment gives you patience. This is the mind of God.

677. Commitment can even save the sinner and lead you to Heaven.

678. People will always remember you for who you were, but never for who you are and will be. But the God I serve always knows and remembers you for who

you were, who you are, and will be. That is why He is the God of yesterday, today, and forever.

679. Some people want to be big, yet they are running away because of persecution.

680. Only the weak-minded can be fooled because they have no vision.

681. Ignorance is the key to failure, while knowledge is the key to success.

682. Your humility could be your greatest source of pride.

683. Your love could be your greatest source of hate.

684. Your kindness could be your greatest source of envy.

685. Aspire to inspire before you expire.

686. No matter how strong you are, you will always be weak. No matter how weak you are, you will always be strong. One thing you can do is submit to the omnipotent God.

687. You will find your enemies where your friends are.

688. Your enemies have more value than your friends.

689. Your enemies can prepare you for your future,

while your friends will discourage you about your future.

690. Your enemies are hard workers, while your friends are lazy people.

691. Every man lies, but not every man can correct themselves.

692. Anything built on a lie will never stand.

693. The devil always speaks part truth and part lie. Be careful of the message you are hearing.

694. Truth is not from the mouth; truth is from the heart, either positive or negative.

695. Only light can allow you to see your shadow.

696. If you stand in the dark for too long, you will see through it. It does not mean that it is light. It's just that you blend in it, you have been in it for too long.

697. Observation is the best truth detector. It will allow you to see every rat out of their hiding places.

698. Sometimes you need to leave the soccer fields and stand in the stadium. You will see how everyone is playing dirty. We need Jesus.

699. Reading the Bible helps you with your lifespan.

700. Life has both positive and negative energy. Negative energy can destroy what God has in store for you. Energy is life itself within you. Negative energy drains the lifespan.

701. When you don't know what you are supposed to know, you are resisting God's presence.

702. God doesn't work within time and time can't limit God.

703. Time is not for God; it is for me. Time was given to me to find myself.

704. Anytime I don't understand something, faith will not remain. Anything God tells you that you don't understand will not come to pass.

705. The only way to overcome your enemies is to accept and pay the price. Otherwise, you will go back and forth with them. They must kill you and you must trust God to bring you back from the dead. Once that happens, they will leave you alone. Kill you means to destroy your reputation, name, business, finances, emotions, and more. They will try to make sure no one wants to help you and turn your own family against you. They will disqualify you and try to break your marriage, friendships, partnerships, and any support. You may end up homeless, jobless, and in a state of nakedness. They may even physically abuse, threaten,

or try to murder you. But if you trust in God through it all and survive, they will eventually leave you alone.

706. There are three levels to preaching. The first one is preaching to yourself. If you can't preach yourself, you can't preach. Once you have preached yourself and are convinced of the word of God, then you can preach to people. And once they are convinced of the word of God, you can preach Jesus Christ.

707. When certain people attack you, it's a message, not a problem. But if you're still alive in your old self, then it becomes a problem.

708. People's words can be like a sword, and if you pay attention to them, they will cut you.

709. Wherever you are in life, there will always be someone who doesn't like you.

710. Don't look back, just keep moving forward. If you take a shortcut, you may die in it.

711. Some people want to embrace the power but forget about the source.

712. If the angel of the Lord walks with me, it means I have been through hell.

713. If you tell me about your hell, I will tell you about the power within you.

714. Don't be like a wild goat. Goats fight with their shepherds and become rebellious.

715. You cannot worship God and mammon at the same time. Money, jobs, and work are part of a system. Don't let money or anyone with money control you.

716. Some people sell their souls. It's not everyone you connect with, follow, or listen to.

717. Your soul is what gives you the ability to choose. Don't engage in certain conversations that may affect your soul.

718. You need someone who will tell you the truth with wisdom. Truth without wisdom is destructive.

719. The wise can learn even from the unlearned.

720. The higher I go, those who shoot at me cannot reach me.

721. Life is in your heart. You must protect yourself so that life can flow within you.

722. Life in me has to do with education and the things known and spoken.

723. The more we understand, the more life comes to us.

724. The more good deeds you do, the more life comes inside of you.

725. The body releases energy from the life inside of us.

726. The quickest way to gain faith is to believe in a Man of God who can teach you.

727. Lazy people cannot receive from God because they lack energy.

728. When you see something and don't have the strength to handle it, it can destroy you.

729. There's no way you can smell good without realizing how bad you smell.

730. You can't become righteous if you were never a sinner.

731. If you didn't have a terrible past, you will not have a great future.

732. If you didn't mess up, you wouldn't know what needs fixing.

733. If you didn't realize you have bad breath, you wouldn't know you have pride. Pride is like a bad breath; everyone can smell it but you.

734. If you weren't dirty, the blood wouldn't have cleansed you.

735. The negative didn't destroy you; it built you.

736. Knowledge of good and evil is what we eat, and how we live.

737. Man loves to justify themselves so they can do what they wants to do.

738. If you are following what others are doing, God is not within you.

739. What you preach is what you have learned from what you have been through.

740. Nothing just happens. Someone has to make it happen. Even for God to change the world, He had to become human.

741. You cannot choose faith. Faith chooses you.

742. To repent means to go back to the cross.

743. No one can get to faith until they have someone they believe in.

744. When people don't spend time with God, they judge others.

745. It's hard to believe in someone because they are human, just like you.

746. If you don't know how to embrace your past, it will destroy you.

747. You don't have a gift; YOU ARE a gift.

748. When you're jealous of someone, you degrade yourself.

749. Overcome yourself, and you will be able to overcome everything.

750. When God makes you a promise, you cannot reason with how He's going to do it.

751. Anointing that can't be traced is witchcraft.

752. If you know your rights, you know your power.

753. The bigger the process, the bigger the blessing.

754. If your worship depends on your happiness, you are not there yet.

755. We must learn to give God a towdah praise no matter how tired we may be... sacrificial praise!

756. It's in the pain that you find the revelation.

757. Where there is vision, is where you invest.

758. Growth is not reading, preaching, or prophesying. It is changing. If the words don't reach you, the power will never touch you.

759. The good Shepherd picks you according to your failures, not to your success.

760. God is so proud that it cost Him humanity to prove He is God!

761. Walk with those who are wise.

762. There is no such thing as "enemies." They are called "distractions," distractions that can hold you from reaching your destiny.

763. It's not by works that God blesses you, but it's by grace that God blesses you.

764. In the world, it's called "Risk" but in the Kingdom of God, it's called "Faith."

765. If you don't increase in knowledge and understanding, you can't keep your commitment.

766. Repentance is a gift from God, not judgment.

767. God always gives to a willing spirit.

768. The habits of a great man make him great.

769. When God releases something to you, don't always look at material things. Look at it spiritually, not naturally.

770. Your greatest enemy is yourself.

771. When hunger meets with the prophetic, solutions happen!

772. Persecution is education!

773. When a religious person says God wants to use you, in reality, they are saying they want to control you.

774. Whenever faith enters you, it opens the calendar of God for you.

775. Faith alone does not fulfill prophecy. You need a sound mind as well.

776. A man with many rules and laws can be easily aggravated and irritated, becoming destructive to others.

777. A man with no rules but love can easily live peacefully and be understandable to others.

778. To reach the level you want to go, you have to start from the bottom.

779. In the vision is the lifeline (soul) of the man. If you know the vision, you will know the man.

780. The greatest education does not happen at school. It happens at home.

781. Education has to do with creativity. Man did not invent cars or airplanes. They discovered it. They saw a bird fly and a horse run, and they said they would make one like it. Man does not invent. They are inspired by what God has already created.

782. Stay away from gossip if you want to be educated.

783. A man who doesn't know his femininity will never keep a good marriage.

784. In a family, it's the mother who teaches. The father instructs the mother. Only a husband can turn a woman into a wife.

785. Too many people are already good at saying the wrong things. Don't go with the trend. Be different, and speak good things.

786. Someone who deserves a gift is someone who works for it.

787. The riches of God is not how much you save. It is how much He provides for you every day.

788. All the hurt and suffering you went through couldn't kill you because God's plan for you felt better than how they feel. Your dreams outweigh your pain.

789. People who don't stand for something will fall for everything.

790. A twisted tongue does not lie. Their lie is true to them.

791. Where there is manipulation, there is witchcraft.

792. When you run out of words, you run out of life.

793. When you don't submit your mind to the word of God, something else will use it.

794. A man full of words is a man full of power.

795. If there is a word, there's a revelation. Everything that we are is a word.

796. Even when you know where you are going, never get ahead of yourself. You will waste your time.

797. God doesn't choose who you marry. If God has to choose for you, then the person is married to God, not you.

798. Remember, the Christian walk is about endurance, not length.

799. Without problems, there's no growth.

800. A worldly person cannot say a Christian is lost because they didn't find something, they are trying everything. A cult or other religion cannot say a Christian is lost because something is using them and destroying them. They didn't find anything. Christianity is to find life and eternal life.

801. Someone may be more talented than you, more anointed than you, more gifted than you. Never let them be more kind than you. Goodness is the greatest talented gift anointing combined.

802. If anything can work without God, then there's something higher than God.

803. The script of life is already written.

804. It's not having money that makes you rich. Richness and blessings come from understanding how life works.

805. Your soul is the filter of the body. It's through your soul that we understand revelation.

806. The greatest number in the spirit is 1. There is One God.

807. Just because someone is intimate doesn't mean they can get pregnant.

808. Someone who is of the flesh cannot give birth. Someone who is of the flesh will copy someone else's idea.

809. In order for me to produce, production does not happen without compassion.

810. God doesn't give you money. He shows you how to make money.

811. Prayer doesn't give you power. It gives you understanding.

812. Your prayer should always be speaking the promises of God over your life.

813. Continue to walk in pride. There's a humble... no name... a young child... a nobody God is raising up to replace you. Before a fall, pride comes.

814. There are some battles that no one can overcome for you.

815. There are some battles, but prayer doesn't do it... you must face it!

816. When I'm spiritual, I can't live by the sword. I have to live by the spirit.

817. The anointing is a license that's given to you when you walk in righteousness. Power without righteousness is illegal.

818. Be careful who you look down on and laugh at. When they finally come up, you will be part of their testimony. Without you, they could not have made it out.

819. No one can preach Christ until they are free.

820. Understanding the sacrifice of Christ means I'm following the steps to conquer or receive power.

821. They supported worse. Don't you dare give up

because of what they are saying? They may have people on their side. Keep God on your side.

822. There are people you want to give precious things to and they will throw it away as if it means nothing. Don't give your pearls to pigs.

823. For some of you, it's not that God cannot use you. You don't understand the value of the Holy Ghost.

824. There must be a difference between the righteous and the wicked. That difference was the blood. The blood gives you the image of Christ.

825. The word PENTECOST means 50. Fifty days after the Passover, the Holy Ghost came down.

826. God does not visit people any day. There are special times when God visits you. He comes to your house.

827. It's not everybody that's been given Pentecostal power.

828. After Pentecost, the last movement of God is the prophetic. "I will pour out my spirit on all flesh, and they will dream dreams, they will have visions, they will prophesy."

829. People who are Pentecostal don't understand the prophetic movement. People who are Baptist don't

understand the Pentecostal movement. People who are Catholic don't understand the Baptist movement.

830. You have the prophetic. No weapon formed against you shall prosper because you have the eye of the eagle on you.

831. If man had the power to choose man, they would have never been fair. But Lord, you have the power. You choose who you want. You appoint who you want.

832. A lot of people know the scriptures, but that does not mean they have power. The power is in the Holy Spirit.

833. A spirit can attack you when you are weak. Being weak doesn't mean you are destroyed.

834. Unlocking power within without the Holy Spirit is witchcraft.

835. Anyone who cannot trust themselves will never be able to trust the Holy Spirit.

836. Koah means abilities. Exousia means possessing authority and the right of rulership. Authority submits to authority.

837. Dunamis' great miraculous power. You need Dunamis to encounter false power that's coming against what you're supposed to do.

838. Kratos means dominion. Iskus means strength. Without the strength to praise Him, you can't love Him. Energia means effectiveness (superhuman power).

839. Time spent with God is time getting to know yourself as well. You don't lose anything spending time with God.

840. When you are alone time with The Lord, the voices that speak in your mind are illegal aliens that God is exposing to you.

841. Time spent with God is not only a gain for power and blessing but also a way to get to know yourself.

842. Prayer can serve as a self-check and a reminder to be obedient every time you resist something that could lead you away from righteousness or the Lord.

843. During prayer, there's spiritual soap, body wash, shampoo, toothbrush, and toothpaste. By the time you finish, you should feel spiritually cleansed.

844. Everyone will be tested by fire. Those who currently laugh at you will walk in your shoes one day. They may either do worse or better. The rotation of the earth stops for no one.

845. Be cautious of church journalists. They are always searching for the next story to expose. They may have successful careers, wealth, nice cars, great marriages,

wonderful families, and strong support systems. However, they also carry bitterness inside and can be ruthless in their pursuit of destruction.

846. Repentance is not about condemnation or judgment. It is about finding eternal life.

847. Don't wait for others to acknowledge you, just keep moving forward. They will never give you a compliment because they fail to recognize anything good that comes from you. All they see is an opportunity to judge you for a mistake. Remember, you will be fine without their compliments. If God is for you, who can be against you?

848. This era... This generation... People don't support or help what God is raising up. But they support or help what they are raising up. They like what they can control, not what God is controlling.

849. Wherever you see temptation, life is there. Wherever you see life, the temptation is there.

850. Sometimes God will keep you in a dry place to protect you. Blessed is the man that endures.

851. Sometimes you're looking for the blessing when you're the blessing.

852. It's not money that makes you rich. It's the gift on the inside that makes you rich.

853. There are some blessings, don't worry about them. When it's not God that gives it to you it will destroy you.

854. God does not do the work for you. He provides the tools for us to do the work.

855. There are some things you reject, automatically power downloads on the inside of you.

856. There are some things you walk away from, automatically power downloads on the inside of you.

857. The only time to wait on God is when you need an instruction or revelation from Him.

858. Someone who celebrates success it's because they didn't deserve it.

859. The source of our life is in the hands of God. The source of our provision is in the hands of God.

860. You must suffer as a Christian. When you suffer as a Christian your provision comes when people look down on you.

861. As time passes, it's harder for people to believe what was.

862. God is eternal… no beginning and no end. We are eternal as He is eternal.

863. God knows the plans He has for us. He just sent us to fulfill the plans.

864. The Bible says we must number our days. If you die before your time, there is a problem.

865. Our days are numbered because we are away from Him. We die quickly because we are away from Him.

866. Where we are is in the realm of Alpha and Omega. It has a beginning point and an ending point.

867. Every time I invest time, something comes to me.

868. Chronos is the measurement of time following a beginning point and an endpoint. Everyone alive lives in Chronos.

869. Kairos is a moment in time when you shine. Kairos is an appointed time. I must pay my Chronos to reach my Kairos.

870. In the anointing you manifest but in the glory you create.

871. Freedom isn't a feeling. Freedom is a change of pattern.

872. The devil makes mistakes for you to get promoted. You make mistakes so God can be glorified.

873. You don't run from your enemies. You go around your enemies to learn what they are doing.

874. A good cheese and wine; When the process is done right, it releases flavors, aromas, and colors. The cheese never gave up; it was once milk.

875. Maturity is not knowing something. It's going through some things.

876. You've got to allow yourself to be broken. Suffering doesn't mean you are extinct.

877. When I come of age, I enter a place where I am existing. Before maturity, you have no purpose. Before maturity, you have no assignment. When I come of age, I leave a legacy.

878. The knowledge of God is in the pain you endure.

879. Prayer doesn't give you power, it gives you direction.

880. What is the cost of eternal life? Let go of everything and follow Him.

881. The mystery of God is a revelation of Christ. An angel is a revelation.

882. Wisdom is the ability to get out of trouble.

883. The wisdom of the earth comes from self-seeking or jealousy.

884. A sorcerer kills someone with the words of their mouth.

885. When you end up pleasing people you're going to do sorcery.

886. Some people are educated preachers, not anointed preachers.

887. Anyone who lies to you and you believe that lie, you are a slave to them.

888. Never celebrate power and manifestations. Celebrate relationship and intimacy.

889. Something wicked under the sun… Someone can hate you because you have the title of a prophet. Then in a few months, they became a prophet and didn't hate themselves because of the title. Wicked!

890. Live as if Jesus is not coming for a long time but work as if He's coming tomorrow.

891. Someone who is fatherless is someone who will suffer greatly in life.

892. What makes a retreat or trip fun is not what you do in it. It's the people that you are with that make it fun.

893. There is a season when God increases you. It's called the seed of God. If God is sowing you have to flush.

894. Spiritual checkups can be done every day. Without it, there would be no self-control.

895. If your conscience is not talking to you the Holy Spirit will stop talking too. Your conscience tells you right from wrong.

896. A spiritual checkup has to be done before midnight. Once midnight hits, another day starts. Whatever you carry into a new day becomes a covenant.

897. Spiritual pipes are your senses. When your senses have been contaminated, you can't serve God.

898. You can't get far from knowing the word and not knowing Christ. There's no power.

899. Innerman is the version of you inside. Outerman is the version of you outside. The inner man represents the genuine you. The outside must be consistent with the inside. The exterior has to be transformed.

900. To experience the power of God you need love. As a Christian, it's not an eye for an eye. Those with a pure heart shall see God.

901. The donkey is an animal of service which represents the gift of the man.

902. Whenever we leave the gift behind, we get into trouble. Whenever we leave the assignment behind, we get into trouble.

903. Culture and traditions are not the Bible.

904. Stick to uniqueness. It's not popular, and it's not a trend. No one will have to compete with you on it. Everyone is not doing it. Be simple and original.

905. Poverty has its own technology. It's called witchcraft and voodoo.

906. Preachers are not supposed to be retiring. You are supposed to be poured out.

907. When the prophets stop prophesying, the people will start guessing about hearing God's voice, leading to the point of teaching false doctrines and apostasy.

908. I realize there's a lot of confusion in the church. It's not because there's no teaching, but because there's no vision. Where there's no vision, the people perish. Many carry the title of prophets, but they don't prophesy, to expose the works of hell, or to reveal the plans and will of God.

909. Prophets now don't prophesy until they see money in the house. They will only prophesy on 3 to 4 people maximum in a room full of people. This is not the Old Testament. It's the New Testament...we receive the spirit without measure.

910. A ministry with money is a blessing from God. But the money that controls ministry is destructive to souls. Be wise. Which comes first, the ministry or the money?

911. Poverty attracts demons. Too much money attracts demons.

912. When God becomes your portion, you manage things better.

913. It is rare to turn what was rejected into a masterpiece. If you take a son you put him in a house, he will be calm but if you take a slave you put him in a house and they will become greedy.

914. The best lessons are when you learn by yourself.

915. If you need a good testimony, you need a new faith.

916. We have been saved by grace because of faith. If faith had never shown up to me, grace would have never applied to me.

917. The King of kings cannot show himself to you unless He's already convinced you.

918. You can resist Jesus, but you cannot resist faith. Having faith means you kidnapped something from God.

919. When faith comes into your life, it comes to work. Lazy people cannot have faith.

920. Science exists to reveal that I'm limited. Whatever results they've gotten, I can reach beyond that.

921. Ministry is not something you know how to do. It's something you were sent to do. If I was sent to do it that means that I'm in constant communication with Him.

922. To fight the impossible, you need the impossible. That's faith!

923. Wherever your intentions or motives are, that's where you are.

924. If you're going to sacrifice, sacrifice to the things of God.

925. You can have salvation here and lose eternal salvation.

926. Blessed speaks of an inner state of well-being and

the prosperity of our soul. Someone can be rich and they're not blessed.

927. A blessing keeps my connection with God.

928. The presence of God is peace…it's gentle…it's love.

929. The ungodly always have something to say. The godly always waits until God has something to say.

930. Perfection in this world is not good. It is evil.

931. Anointing you want to look like, if that anointing is not traceable, it is witchcraft.

932. Rivers are revelations. Revelations come from the word of God.

933. In the first stage of Christianity, you are looking for a taste. You've tried everything out there because you're looking for satisfaction.

934. The grace of God deals with the Holy Spirit. The grace of God can be as a favor.

935. With the grace of God, He doesn't need your permission. Grace is not defined by works.

936. When you understand the grace of God, you stop boasting, you let go of certain things like anger.

937. God graces you with certain abilities that most don't have. In grace, there are supernatural abilities.

938. Someone who boasts or brags is someone who will embarrass you around people.

939. It's not how fast you can win the battle, it's how much you can learn from the battle. Because there will be many battles.

940. Your greatest encouragement is going to come from you.

941. If you are too happy with what you work so hard for, you don't deserve it. That is why I get happy when God uses me for salvation or in an encounter with God. But never for a house, a car, money, or material things. My happiness in having Christ is enough that I deserve everything else because of Him.

942. Don't grow too fast or you will fall faster.

943. While they are trying to show they are capable, you push to be successful. Don't compete with their capabilities.

944. It only takes one day for your status to change from poverty to prosperity.

945. Prayer doesn't give power or make you strong. Prayer searches the insides of you.

946. Doctrine is translated into instruction. It applies to a way or a lifestyle. We are one body but have different instructions. When doctrine is attacked the foundation is attacked.

947. You must be able to defend your faith, not your emotions, and not your ambitions.

948. If you look for problems you will always find one. It's hard to find solutions.

949. A lot of people have the calling of God, but not a lot of people can sustain the calling of God.

950. If God has to send you somewhere that's already prepared, you are only a copy! You are not original.

951. Loyalty does not need to understand what you are doing to be loyal.

952. There is a grace and anointing that God gives to someone; it's not for people who are healed. It's for people who are sick.

953. Troubles don't stop, it's the peace that stops. People fight to keep their peace. They don't fight to keep their troubles.

954. The confidence of our hope is a confident expectation.

955. Hope can't be hope if it is known. You have to hope for something that does not exist.

956. The confession of my faith DEFINES me, but the confession of my hope DEMONSTRATES me.

957. Some people are rich internally, but externally, they're poor.

958. Anyone who can start something and not finish it, there is a battle within them that they have not yet overcome.

959. Never let what's in your mind download into your heart. Don't let your heart change. When you're reading the word of God, what is within you (trash) will come out, and God will deal with it.

960. If God gives it to you too early, you can become like the prodigal son. The prodigal son wasted all of his riches and had to eat with pigs.

961. Become more transparent as you read the word of God. Don't be afraid to expose yourself in order to grow.

962. Growth is beautiful. Don't doubt the power of growth.

963. Reading the word exposes things around you and within you and tells you where you're supposed to be.

964. Many people are gifted. But if you function in that gift without God, you can turn into a warlock or witch.

965. Gifts are good. But it's not wise to work with gifts without a relationship.

966. Some do not fear God. Fear of God will cause you to have limitations in your life. Don't ever let God be the one to discipline you.

967. Worship is very important. Worship has nothing to do with voice. It would not be fair for God to give to some and not others.

968. God is seeking true worshipers. When God's army is going to war, it was the Levites that were chosen, not the warriors.

969. To become a true worshiper, I need to understand the word of God or it can become a destruction in my life. You must walk in the spirit, and live in the spirit.

970. You cannot be praying in tongues without the scriptures. You have to understand the word of truth. In the spiritual realm, what protects is the word of God.

971. To worship it comes with honor, reverence, fear, and respect. You can't worship God if you can't honor Him. You can't worship God if you don't revere Him. You can't worship God if you don't fear Him. You can't worship God if you don't respect Him.

972. Honor is something I see! No one had to teach me or tell me. When you give God the honor, it is revealed to you. It pushes you to honor Him. If you can't see that, your worship is powerless. Some people worship God because of something they want. Never do that!

973. Most test the spirit by the spirit. You have to have the right spirit to test the spirit. How do I test the spirit? I test it by the word of God.

974. The more you study the word of God, the more spiritual infiltrates the physical.

975. You can pray all you want in the spirit but if your natural state is not right, you're not going to get what you want.

976. No matter how many people are around you, your journey with God is always lonely.

977. Loneliness means God is taking you on a journey. There is something you have to fulfill.

978. You can have the money and you're still not approved.

979. It's the blessing that's on the inside that counts.

980. Be slow to speak! Sometimes, people want you to say certain words because they want your birthright.

981. Someone who loses their birthright hates people who still have theirs.

982. When God saves you and gives you something and you sell it, you are in a danger zone.

983. Don't sell your birthright, even if you're hungry.

984. Your obsession should be The Lord's presence. Then you will see everything else fall into place.

985. A gift doesn't mean God is using you. There's more to it... A gift is a bonus of grace when God is using you.

986. Without a purpose, you will be a copycat.

987. Behind a strong man, there's a humble and wise woman. Two strong individuals don't make it better.

988. If you love people, you will hear God every day.

989. Never cut off people who know you for those who don't and have to learn all about you again.

I understand that the more problems you go through with someone and survive, the more understanding develops between you and that person. You don't have to constantly change friends, just endure the challenges. Don't be an opportunist. There are individuals who only go where they feel most comfortable but solely use people for their own benefit. Such individuals are destined to fail, never find success, and will never receive honor and love.

990. Prayer can be converted to energy and strength but you need to have energy and strength to give.

991. The power of prayer is not supernatural. It depends on how much understanding the person praying has.

If prayer is a language, just like English and Creole are languages...

If it is a language, I communicate through it and it helps people...

So when I pray, I communicate with God on behalf of someone, and it all depends on the strength and understanding I have to help that person when I pray...

The prayer of a righteous person is effective…

992. The Kingdom of God chooses people who are weak. The worse your past is, the more he wants to use you.

993. The Kingdom of God is the rulership, the Kingship of Jesus in the hearts of man.

994. Church people talk more about exposing people than restoring them.

We can't be the accuser of the brethren - that title doesn't belong to any Christian.

995. A lack of discernment is a lack of power. Peeping is not discernment.

996. The act of faith is rare because it's been classified as witchcraft.

997. People on the sidelines think they know more than the people on the field. The bystanders think they can play better than the team.

998. Saul was bound by the law.

Paul was freed from the law.

999. Someone who's not redeemed will condemn you for what you're doing because they themselves have not been saved. They have a limitation.

1000. The redeemed of God is someone who's been broken. God took them through the fire and a process that crushed every bone in their body.

1001. Love is a personality, not a feeling. Love doesn't build a marriage. Love is universal. Anyone can love it.

1002. One thing about the sun is that it does its job every day. The sun doesn't wake up one day and say, "There's going to be clouds, so they won't see me, so I'm not going to shine." Clouds or not, it shines.

That is your problem - you worry about what's trying to cover you. You stop shining because they're on the way.

1003. A plague comes because there is a disturbance in the history of things. Whenever we see signs of plague it means God wants to bless his people.

1004. God uses your imperfection to declare His perfection.

1005. Worship is the only thing that moves God.

1006. The pattern and path to growth is submission. You will never know righteousness until you accept righteousness. Tradition is not righteousness.

1007. You cannot have zeal solely based on desire; it has to be rooted in knowledge to avoid falling into error.

1008. Anointing you don't pay for is just a feeling.

1009. A prayer that has no direction is a prayer that has confusion.

1010. When a tree is growing, leaves have to fall. It doesn't mean the tree is dying. It reaches a point where the leaves have to produce fruit.

1011. The soul gives you the power to make decisions. That is why Satan can't take your soul until you give it to him.

1012. With God, there is no dead end. If you reach a dead end, He will give you the opportunity to construct new roads.

1013. The word can't become alive until there's pain. That's when it becomes real.

1014. The power of God comes through a great mind. The more I can keep my mind clean the more I can create.

1015. The thing you are praying the most about is what the enemy is coming after. That's why when we pray we must be led into prayer.

1016. What makes us is not perfection; it's because we are human. Sometimes you can make mistakes and that's what God is looking for so He can show His power.

1017. God is the true image of us. We are the copy. You cannot get help from God if you think you're the original.

1018. Some things don't need prayer. Certain things need decisions.

1019. The image we talk about is not the flesh. The image we talk about is the image of Glory.

1020. We were made in the image of Christ. If we don't walk in that image all the powers that are stored in that image won't be functional.

1021. Truth becomes truths by trials. False becomes false because it couldn't stand the trials. ARE YOU TRUE OR FALSE??

1022. For something to be true, it has to be tested.

1023. A lie is not the opposite of truth. It's something that wants to appear to be true.

1024. When the test comes it exposes what is real and what is not real.

1025. If you can't listen, your waters will turn bitter.

1026. The righteous will fall seven times. The number 7 stands for completion which means fall until you get it right.

1027. The longer you last the more revelation you receive. If you fall don't quit, get back up again.

1028. The biggest secret of ministry is endurance.

1029. Most want to go find the answer instead of the answer coming to you.

1030. If you take in someone who is lost and give them what they need...they will honor you more than someone who has been found and you are taking care of.

1031. A lost dog will always be more grateful for a good home than a dog that's been in a good home.

1032. There are the obstacles and there's what matters. You will always find the problem, but what matters comes with sense, understanding, vision, and sight.

1033. If worldly music can calm you down, how much more will worshiping God affect you?

1034. God took away Saul's ability to worship. Worship is the access to God.

Saul lost access to worship and because of that, he could not find his way to God.

1035. If you want your heart to remain pure, learn how to worship.

1036. Hate does not have a destination. But love has a destination.

1037. If Daniel can survive in the lion's den then I can survive around people.

1038. The word of God is the only thing that can line up your DNA to what God wants you to be.

1039. One shouldn't rely on someone else's testimony to receive faith. This is how one makes mistakes.

1040. Wisdom doesn't come from tomorrow. Wisdom comes from yesterday.

1041. You are who you are because of yesterday not because of tomorrow. It was yesterday that built you, not tomorrow.

1042. To inherit eternal life is to enter the Kingdom of God. Some will make it there but they won't inherit the Kingdom.

1043. It's not the priests, it's not the Levites that will inherit the Kingdom of God. It's the Samaritans.

1044. The remote control didn't need to see the TV once there was a connection. As long as there's a connection, the remote is not too far away. It will sense the TV and you can change to any channel. In the same way, you don't need to see God to be used by God. You only need a connection, that's it. As long as you stay close to Him, you will sense Him.

1045. If your journey did not turn into an adventure, you fail in life.

1046. There's no need to trust if it wasn't difficult. That's why trust is required because it's hard and challenging. If you're looking for something easy that you can trust, it will deceive you and turn against you. It's the difficult things that need trust.

1047. A goat that has a lot of masters will eventually die.

1048. Staying in your lane is the best decision you can make in life.

1049. Only a King can make a king.

1050. There's a stage in life that does not require effort. Sometimes it only requires presence.

1051. If you have no regrets about the past, you need to be grateful because you become a better person. If you have regrets, you are still the same person. You are ungrateful.

1052. If you're able to take the righteousness of God then you will see abilities in you that have never been discovered.

1053. Someone who walks in righteousness is a King in front of wickedness.

1054. We are collective knowledge. Without your neighbor there is something that's missing.

1055. When people you know, friends or family, win, it's a beautiful thing, not a jealous thing. Learn to celebrate winners, not be jealous of them.

1056. Some people are bridges. You need them to crossover.

1057. The devil makes mistakes so we can be promoted. My mistakes are so God can be glorified. Therefore, you never lose!

1058. Your greatest blessing is inside that pain. You have to endure it! Success comes with pain. Anyone who can survive the pain... expansion!

1059. The way you think says where you're going and what's going to happen to you.

1060. Success comes with problems. I rather suffer when succeeding than suffer while failing. If I'm suffering while succeeding there's discipline. It means I'm suffering on purpose.

1061. We are running the race for a prize.

What's worth more? The trophy or the winner?

1062. Sometimes winning or success can cause you more damage than losing or failure. Make sure you are ready for it, or else it could potentially be the end of you.

1063. Love being humble...because you don't have to carry the weight of showing off or proving yourself to people.

1064. Some people have to go ahead of you so that they can tell people about you. Just because they went ahead of you, doesn't mean you're late.

1065. Growth doesn't happen when I hear. Growth happens when I make the change.

1066. Sometimes it's better to die than to rot in prison.

1067. Dreams cannot come to pass unless you are captured. When you have the gift, the potential, and the dream and you get comfortable, you will end up in jail.

1068. The prison is the place where you start dreaming. They say it's in the cage that the mockingbird sings.

1069. God hates it when people get comfortable. The moment you become comfortable, you kill your skills.

1070. There are some battles, if you face them, you will be killed. Sometimes, use your brain and walk away. Let them laugh…

1071. When you know where you are going, there are some battles you don't fight.

1072. Someone who is a visionary will always look stupid in front of those who have no vision.

1073. It's people who don't have grace who hate.

Millionaires don't worry about people who don't have money.

1074. What makes someone human is how they respect people. Anyone who cannot respect people is an animal.

1075. Someone who has been saved, justified, and set free from sin can still fail, but they can also rise again. Failure is a gift, but it's a gift to get it right.

1076. We are the only beings in the universe that can fail and still be successful.

God can't fail…

Jesus cannot fail…

Angels cannot fail…

Satan already failed and was condemned for it.

1077. Failing is a gift from God. If you hate failing, you reject God's gift to you.

1078. There's going through it, and there's being in it. Both of them feel the same way, but the difference is that you come out of one of them.

1079. When you're going through your process, are you blessed enough for your strength to be in God? It's a privilege!

1080. Everything you go through has to be equal to a blessing.

1081. If you fail to appreciate the work of others, you will not be able to draw from a greater level of anointing than what you currently see.

1082. There are a couple of things that can make someone look stupid and get them into trouble:

-Talking too much

-Showing off

-Acting like they know everything

-Moving too fast

-Getting involved in too many things

-Always wanting to be on top

1083. The outcome of the process will put you on higher ground.

1084. People who are scared to get embarrassed will never be able to receive a blessing.

1085. Just because someone doesn't understand your path doesn't mean you should change your pattern.

1086. Blessing comes with pain. Any blessing that doesn't have pain in it isn't a blessing.

1087. People believe God doesn't have power because they are moving too fast.

1088. It doesn't matter how gifted you are; you still need time.

1089. Anyone who doesn't read the bible and meditate on the word has a dirty soul.

1090. Prayer is like glue for your soul, body, and spirit. Without it, everything will crash.

1091. If it's not their story, they may not care to listen. That is why when you make it historic, they will have no choice but to remember it.

1092. No matter how powerful you think you are, you can never play the position of God.

1093. The more anointing that comes, the more you have to humble yourself. The more people that come around, the more alone you get.

1094. You could be anyone when people don't know you, but you can only be yourself when everyone knows your story.

It's better for man to judge you than for God to judge you…

1095. If you don't understand someone's flaws, they can be anyone to you. If someone looks perfect, be afraid of them…

1096. Someone can also be transparent, but they may use their failures as a way of manipulation to justify wrong as right.

1097. You can only become transparent to become right not to remain wrong.

1098. When you've got nothing to lose, God is your provider and your defense.

1099. Man will judge you based on your flaws, but God will help and use you despite your flaws. God loves to use trash as art.

1100. Only someone who cannot fight needs to defend themselves. Because those who can fight have already endured countless beatings to learn how to fight, and have grown accustomed to the pain. They no longer feel the need to fight. Instead, they become superheroes who help others.

1101. It's worse when God disciplines you than when man disciplines you.

1102. It's not easy to be successful. It's easy to fail. Being successful comes with regulations. To fail comes with whatever.

1103. Someone has to teach you so you can teach somebody else. If you never got that teaching, you would live a sinful life.

1104. With any business you get into, you have a contract to deal with.

1105. There are things you see, hear, and know in people's lives, but you are not on a level to deal with them. It will destroy you!

1106. Don't blame God for hell. It wasn't made by him.

1107. If you didn't convince yourself about your dreams, then you still don't believe you can fulfill them.

1108. If you have something good going for you, do not let it go even if you make mistakes.

Transform persistence into perfection.

1109. Not every battle is essential to winning... It's ok to lose some battles... Just make sure you win the war.

1110. An open heaven cannot happen individually. It's a connection. It's collective knowledge.

1111. If it's only you that receive, it's not an open heaven; it's a grace.

1112. An open heaven only happens with something

you haven't seen before. You have to change your pattern. You have to have a new encounter.

1113. When God is on your side, never back down!

1114. There is a level of grace that cannot be explained; you have to be there for yourself.

1115. Your battle is your battle. God will only give you the tools. You fight for it!

1116. NEVER REPLY TO CRITICISM OR YOU WILL LOSE... NOT LOSING AGAINST THE CRITICS, BUT LOSING YOUR FOCUS, LOSING YOUR PLANS, LOSING YOUR HEART DESIRE... THE CRITICISM OF THE CRITIC WAS NOT MEANT TO BE A BATTLE, BUT TO GET YOUR ATTENTION ON WHAT YOU ARE BUILDING.

1117. There's nothing to prove to anyone when I know who I am.

1118. There's a revelation God gave you that doesn't fit where you are.

1119. Patience is a gift. HOPE when you do not murder.

1120. The pain of patience is labor pain. Eventually, it will give birth.

1121. It's that simple: IF YOU DON'T KNOW GOD'S WILL, YOU WILL HAVE NO IDEA WHAT YOUR PURPOSE IN LIFE IS.

1122. Will and purpose are twins. It's so simple.

1123. Everyone lies, but not everyone is a liar.

1124. When my mind runs, it means prayer time.

1125. When I overthink, it means prayer time.

1126. Peace means that even if I see what hurts me, it doesn't hurt me anymore because I've overcome it.

1127. Stop asking God for a blessing and recognize that you are the blessing.

1128. Out of hatred, they killed Jesus. It is dangerous when someone hates you. Out of hatred, Cain killed Abel. Hate is a force of evil that gives power to do what righteousness does not agree with or what love doesn't support.

1129. Your lifeline is the savings account you have for whatever it is. When something goes wrong, you can go there to restore it. It's in everything that's important in your life or to you. YOU NEED A LIFE LINE... Without a lifeline, it will be destroyed.

1130. The will of God has many different possibilities, but He chooses what He wants in it.

1131. Your will is inside God's will. It's whatever He ordained. You can't do anything outside of that.

1132. The grace of God is what you could have done that will not work. But it's what He could've done that will always work.

1133. It's people who have knowledge of His existence who can manipulate the word!

1134. THERE IS A DIFFERENCE WHEN YOU ARE NOT GETTING WET AND KNOW IT IS RAINING..... and when you are getting wet and knowing it is raining.... raining.

1135. Someone can be breathing and still be in hell.

1136. A dreamer has access where normal dreamers don't.

1137. When you find out the secret of the enemy, it's easy to destroy it.

1138. You can't be humble or patient if you don't have something to live for and die for.

1139. Every spiritual battle reflects a natural battle.

1140. A FATHER WILL NOT GIVE YOU WHAT YOU WANT. HE WILL GIVE YOU WHAT YOU NEED.

1141. When it comes to your destiny, the enemy doesn't attack where you are going. He attacks what you believe in.

1142. ANYONE WHO KNOWS HOW TO PRAY ARE GREAT BEGGAR. THERE IS ASKING AND THERE IS BEGGING. Deep prayers are begging, not asking.

1143. A goat that has many masters will eventually die.

1144. Your worship does not depend on anyone around you. It depends on your relationship with God.

1145. The keys to maturity are consistency and perseverance in doing the things that we know will draw us closer to God.

1146. Consistency emphasizes faith over experience.

1147. The root of every problem is what you feel. The power of every solution is what you feel.

1148. One of the secrets to Greatness is when people who don't like you celebrate you.

1149. Stop dressing your body. Start dressing your heart.

1150. If you're not walking by the spirit, how can you run? I walk, so I can run.

1151. It's not you who will change people. It's your faith in God.

1152. When you hold onto something or someone, they live rent-free in your life while they live life.

1153. If you can't believe it anymore, you can't see where you are going.

1154. Spirituality is too much without knowledge. Someone who is so spiritual without knowledge is destroying themselves.

1155. You lose social connections with people when you lack physical maturity. 99% of problems people have are their own, not someone else's.

1156. Until your mind is changed, you cannot approve of what is good.

1157. Falling is a gift from God. Without falling, you cannot become successful. You fail to realize that you are human and that you need God to survive.

1158. Growth does not have sight; it just happens.

1159. To make it in life, your mind needs to be sharp like a knife.

1160. You can never love someone unless you see them for who they are.

1161. We are in a constant present. It doesn't change. Our past makes our lives better. Our past makes us who we are today. Our job is to do our best to live now and make the most of it. The future will come, but we are here now.

1162. No one can become great if they cannot submit to someone great.

1163. You did not become a Christian because you saw Christ. You became a Christian because Christ saw you.

1164. Until you work hard, don't expect to receive favors and blessings.

1165. If you can find your heart, you will find heaven. The GPS or address to heaven is you.

1166. Until you receive the gospel of the kingdom, you can never have the inheritance of the Kingdom.

1167. When you are too spiritual, you miss the physical. When you are too physical, you miss the spiritual.

1168. Sometimes you think that the more you have, the more you will gain. When you start losing, it means God is changing things for you.

1169. When the Lord wins your heart, salvation comes to you.

1170. When the Lord wins your mind, you live in heaven on earth.

1171. The more specific the prophetic word is, the harder the process becomes.

1172. When you are inspired by the Spirit, you can never expire!

1173. If you don't know how to follow a Man of God, you can never follow the Holy Spirit. For people who didn't see Jesus face-to-face for a commission, a Man of God who is a covering or a leader is the voice of the Holy Spirit for you.

1174. Learning is not taking it on your own or interpreting it how you want.

1175. TO BE SUCCESSFUL... THE BETTER MIND WINS...

1176. As Christians, we're not supposed to use cell phones. A cell phone is a model of spiritual connection.

1177. It's the type of honor you give that will make people honor you. I can't give you something you do not value or respect.

1178. Someone who prays loudly is someone who doesn't know spiritual road maps.

1179. When you pray loudly, the only thing that can control your mind is the sound of your voice. But someone who has control over their mind doesn't need to speak loudly. They don't need to pray loudly. There is a dimension when you pray; it sounds like whispering.

1180. Anyone who is led by the Holy Spirit has a common factor. It's called hesitation. Before they do anything, there is a pause. Why the hesitation? Because they want to know if the Holy Ghost agrees.

1181. To know oneself is to know the Holy Spirit. You cannot know yourself if you do not know the Holy Spirit.

1182. In ministry, anointing doesn't succeed. MINDS DOES.

1183. You will not be aware of the importance of a tree until the sun beats your head up.

1184. There's no such thing as big sin and little sin. You can't characterize sin. Sin is when you reject God's word.

1185. The people they judge are the people God looks for. If people push you down, God will lift you up.

1186. When you are:

- A LEADER
- A BUSINESS OWNER
- SUCCESSFUL
- SOMEONE PEOPLE LOOK UP TO

You cannot be easily offended by things or people.

1187. You can't run from trials, you must face it. The knowledge of God comes in darkness as well as light.

1188. If we're running a race there are obstacles that will come our way. It's not about the race, it's about finishing.

1189. Anything you give birth to, if it doesn't grow, it will die. That growth comes from you.

1190. If you listen to people, you will fail to listen to GOD.

1191. Faith doesn't require you to work. Faith requires you to see it.

1192. The fact that you are scared of who you are, you cannot be who you're supposed to be.

1193. It's not what you do that defines who you are. It's who you are that defines who you are.

1194. The only way you can be inspired is when you have someone else you look up to. You can only have ideas when you find someone with ideas. Your idea works because you are in a place of vision.

1195. When I have Christ, I do not feel I am in captivity, I feel I am free.

1196. Until you get to the place where you start losing friends, you're not yet a Christian.

1197. You have to get under someone before you have your own. Learn the game before you do the game.

1198. Persecution is education!

1199. To become accountable to God, when He's talking, you stay quiet.

1200. The good news of the Kingdom is that if you accept Jesus, you are not a sinner. But you need to be delivered.

1201. If you have the word, you don't have the spirit, the word will not work. Having the word without the spirit is foolishness.

1202. Your pain is a sign of a new chapter.

1203. They can call you all types of names. They can label you however they want to label you. They can reject you however they want to reject you. But if God is not done with you, no one can stop you.

1204. A soul that has not been convinced of its condition cannot be delivered.

1205. Accept the condition of your soul so someone can bring you out.

1206. It's ok if people laugh at your condition. The laughter is fuel to your prayer life.

1207. It's not about our gifts. It's not about our talents. It's about what we can survive.

1208. There is no weakness or flaw in the message of the Lord.

1209. You don't fight people for what you gave birth to.

1210. There is nothing you start that is yours. But everything you complete is yours.

1211. A wife who honors her husband is worthy of respect.

1212. A wife who honors her husband as a Man of God is worth being honored by others.

1213. Leaders who honor their leaders are worth following.

1214. Leaders who honor their Man of God will become leaders.

1215. Sheep who honor their shepherd will be saved from slaughter.

1216. Sheep who honor their Man of God will live a great life in green pasture.

1217. Honor always honors honor.

1218. Someone who is curious will gossip and will not hurt who they gossip about but who is close to them. Because curiosity has no loyalty.

1219. Intentions and hearts can mess up with discerning. If your intention or heart is not right, discernment won't work.

1220. When you tell someone who has no knowledge of righteousness to be holy, you destroy their mind.

1221. If you did not capture the energy, you did not capture the revelation.

1222. You can't use the word of God without love.

1223. To be a weapon, you are not a weapon to people. You are a weapon against yourself.

1224. I'm a weapon to defend my soul and spirit. My

soul has been bought by Christ. My spirit has been given to him.

1225. There are people who hear the call but don't show up.

1226. Christians have a frequency. They can hear God. A worldly person can't hear.

1227. God uses foolish things. Everyone who will make it to heaven has a weakness by nature.

1228. The power of God is His word.

1229. Prophecy without the Holy Ghost is witchcraft.

1230. It's not easy to follow the invisible God, visible!

1231. In the spirit, you don't count time; you count consistency.

1232. "Until I know within me, I will never know me."

1233. Never base your Christianity on goodness. You will be disappointed.

1234. Without righteousness, no one can see the glory of God in your life. Goodness cannot reflect God's glory!

1235. The best way for me to learn from people is for me to know their purpose.

1236. Never run away from your purpose. Run away from people who have no purpose.

1237. Everyone that exists is a piece of God's knowledge.

1238. You cannot know the word of God by reading it. You can only understand the word of God by listening.

1239. The pain I endured to get the promotion is greater than the pain of being insulted.

1240. When you find your place of promotion, don't give it up. Insults are a sign that you're about to be promoted.

1241. Great people are people who are led by a man who is led.

1242. When God has given you a gift, if you don't love the gift, nobody will love the gift.

1243. Anyone who is not educated substitutes education for emotions.

1244. Without education, you will fail. If you don't like to learn, don't even try to produce wealth.

1245. Someone can be uneducated, but if you understand the word of God, you will succeed.

1246. Anyone who cannot change themselves cannot succeed.

1247. To know if you truly love is to love when those you love hate you. That's when you know you have love.

1248. Learning is a process. Just because you are experiencing things doesn't mean you have learned yet.

1249. An uneducated person is always someone who's trying to show something they never learned or understood. Uneducated is not when you didn't go to school; it's when you are trying to be the loudest at something you don't know, didn't learn, or weren't educated for.

1250. At the same time, just because someone can be so quiet doesn't mean they know because it's a form of deception. Knowledge has to do with when to teach and educate people or help people.

1251. Being educated is not loud at all. It's gentle, not aggressive, not forceful, not deceptive, not manipulative.

1252. When the learning process is complete, an assignment is given.

# KEY WISDOM DEFINITION

**Curiosity** means you are a baby.

**Pride** means you are uneducated.

**Insecurity** means you know everyone but yourself.

**Anger** means you don't know your heart.

**Stubbornness** means you have an imaginary leader.

**Jealousy** means you don't know what's yours.

**Greed** means you're lazy.

**Loneliness** means you've lost yourself.

**Anxiousness** means you know you are a failure.

**Rejection** means you have not accepted yourself.

**Regret** means you only see one part of time—it could be yesterday, today, or tomorrow.

**Sadness** means you lost your essence at creation or birth.

**Depression** means not being a good protector of yourself.

**Pressure** means you're weak.

**Shyness** is the fear of success.

**Frustration** means you need to find help before something worse happens.

**Aggression** is a sign of something worse than frustration.

**Doubt** is losing your sense of self and God.

**Fear** is losing your confidence in purpose and destiny.

**Overprotectiveness** is a self-interest in something specific you want in someone.

Being overprotective of something or someone will eventually get worse. That means when you think you are protecting the person, they will need to be protected from you.

**Lukewarm** is when you don't stand for anything.

The best decisions won't come from what you like; they come from what you're supposed to be doing where you're supposed to be, even if you don't like it.

**Unimportant** is someone who is afraid of what they can do.

**Abused** is caging (limiting) what you can do.

**Indecisiveness** is being confused about what you can do.

**Comfortable**: You stop your growth.

**Lazy**: You are using people.

**Emotionless**: Your soul is bound by something.

The **patient** person makes the faster person get hurt first to learn…

The **slow-to-speak** person makes the person who speaks fast get shamed first before they speak…

The person with **love** lets the angry person act first so they can be the nice person.

A person with a **teachable** spirit makes a stubborn person fight to learn more from the teacher.

The **soft** person makes the hard person fight all their battles.

The person with the **truth** makes the liar show how much we need the truth.

The **humble** person makes them proud and shows how much they need them.

**Righteousness always wins.**

# PROPHETIC DICTIONARY

A **NOSY** person is someone who is using their gift in the wrong way. They were born as an intercessor, but demons have influenced them to become nosy.

**GOSSIPERS** are people who are using their gifts in the wrong way. They were born to evangelize, but demons have influenced them to gossip.

**LIARS** are people who are using their gifts in the wrong way. They were called to speak the truth in people's lives, but demons have made them liars.

**HATERS** are true lovers. The fact that they refuse to love is due to demons influencing them to hate.

**PEOPLE WHO LIKE TO ASSASSINATE OTHERS' CHARACTERS** are using their gifts in the wrong way. They were meant to be blessed people, divine helpers, and divine connections, but demons have influenced them to assassinate others' lives.

**A JEALOUS PERSON** is a true giver, but they are in the wrong field. Due to their failure to submit, demons have made them lazy and jealous of others.

**A PERSON WHO DESTROYS PEOPLE's LIVES** was meant to bless others for life. Blinded by their confidence, they end up causing destruction instead.

# THE STORY OF PRIDE AND SUCCESS

Once upon a time, a mother gave birth to twins, both of them boys. She named one Pride and the other Success. Growing up, Pride was very bold and quick-witted, while Success was skilled and intelligent. One day, a man came by and saw the twins. They both had strong appearances, and he owned a multimillion-dollar company. He needed one of the boys to take over his company, so he decided to test them to see which one would be the best fit.

The first test was a communication skills test. Pride confidently said, "I've got this. It's my specialty, hands down." He spoke with great confidence and impressed the man. On the other hand, Success didn't have much to say. Due to Pride's performance, the man favored him and overlooked Success.

The second test was a skills test. Success demonstrated his capabilities and impressed the owner with his work. The owner confessed that he didn't know Success had such skills. However, when Pride saw the owner's admiration for Success's work, he became unhappy and started speaking loudly to get the owner's attention.

Hearing this, the owner told them to go home and said he would make his decision the next day. He felt a strong connection with Success due to his quiet nature and excellent skills. He believed Success would be someone who could continue his work and listen to him.

In the middle of the night, while everyone was asleep, Pride suddenly killed his twin brother, Success. It was devastating, considering how close they were and how they had done everything together. Pride's actions stemmed from his jealousy over Success potentially inheriting the company, which could have benefited both of them.

When morning came, they discovered Pride sitting on a chair, covered in Success's blood. Pride was immediately arrested and sentenced to spend the rest of his life behind bars. The mother, who had already lost her twins, suffered even more and eventually lost her life as well. She was impoverished and her health deteriorated.

What is the lesson of this story? This story serves as a lesson on the destructive nature of jealousy and greed. It emphasizes that success achieved through unethical means will ultimately lead to ruin and tragedy.